Animals Amigurumi

Amigurumi Crochet Patterns For Beginners

Copyright © 2021

All rights reserved.

DEDICATION

The author and publisher have provided this e-book to you for your personal use only. You may not make this e-book publicly available in any way. Copyright infringement is against the law. If you believe the copy of this e-book you are reading infringes on the author's copyright, please notify the publisher at: https://us.macmillan.com/piracy

Contents

LION AMIGURUMI CROCHET PATTERN 2

SOCK MONKEY AMIGURUMI CROCHET PATTERN ..29

FOX AMIGURUMI PATTERN 51

RACCOON AMIGURUMI PATTERN 69

DEER AMIGURUMI PATTERN 88

ELEPHANT AMIGURUMI CROCHET PATTERN 107

Animals Amigurumi

LION AMIGURUMI CROCHET PATTERN

Materials

- 2.5mm hook
- Acrylic yarn in Yellow, Light Khaki, Dark Brown, Beige and Black colors
- Polyester fiberfill
- 10mm Dome-Button Eye, 1 pair
- 18mm Safety Nose, 1 pc.

Animals Amigurumi

Tools

- Darning needle (Long)
- Fabric marker (water erasable)
- Cardboard, 4"
- Scissors
- Pins

Instructions

1. Crochet all parts by following the crochet patterns stated below.
2. Stuff the parts as instructed
3. For head, sew muzzle on the head after completed round 33, remove stuffing to install safety nose. Re-stuff the head again and continue the pattern to complete the head. Sew dome-button eyes, followed by the ears to the head.
4. Wind yarns to the 4" cardboard. Cut about 1,00 strips of Dark Brown yarns at the length of about 4" as the mane of the lion.
5. Sew body to the head followed by sewing arms, feet and tail to the body
6. Sew the paws line to the arms and feet of the lion.
7. Fasten mane to the head of the lion with the strips cut in #4.

Animals Amigurumi

~ . ~ . ~ . ~ . ~

Abbreviations

ch: chain

sc: single crochet

inc: 2sc incresase

inv dec: invisible decrease

ps3: puff stitch (hdc3tog)

~ . ~ . ~ . ~ . ~

AMIGURUMI PATTERN

Body

With Yellow yarn:

Animals Amigurumi

Round 1: ch5, Inc in 2nd ch from hook, sc 2, 5sc in the last ch. Continue on the other side of the chain base, sc 2, 3sc in the last ch. {14}

Round 2: Inc, sc 4, [Inc] 3 times, sc 4, [Inc] 2 times. {20}

Round 3: Inc, sc 6, [Inc] 2 times, sc, Inc, sc 6, [Inc] 2 times, sc. {26}

Round 4: Inc, sc 8, [Inc, sc] 2 times, Inc, sc 8, [Inc, sc] 2 times. {32}

Round 5: Inc, sc 10, Inc, sc 2, Inc, sc, Inc, sc 10, Inc, sc 2, Inc, sc. {38}

Round 6: Inc. sc 12, [Inc, sc 2] 2 times, Inc, sc 12, [Inc, sc 2] 2 times. {44}

Round 7: Inc, sc 14, Inc, sc 3, Inc, sc 2, Inc, sc 14, Inc, sc 3, Inc, sc 2. {50}

Round 8: Inc, sc 16, [Inc, sc 3] 2 times, Inc, sc 16, [Inc, sc 3] 2 times. {56}

Round 9: sc around. {56}

Round 10: sc 25, Inc, sc 27, Inc, sc 2. {58}

Round 11: sc 26, Inc, sc 28, Inc, sc 2. {60}

Round 12: sc 27, Inc, sc 29, Inc, sc 2. {62}

Round 13: sc 28, Inc, sc 30, Inc, sc 2. {64}

Animals Amigurumi

Round 14 – 23: sc around. {64}

Round 24: sc 6, [Inv dec, sc 14] 3 times, Inv dec, sc 8. {60}

Round 25: sc around. {60}

Round 26: sc 6, [Inv dec, sc 13] 3 times, Inv dec, sc 7. {56}

Round 27: sc around. {56}

Round 28: sc 6, [Inv dec, sc 12] 3 times, Inv dec, sc 6. {52}

Round 29: sc around. {52}

Round 30: sc 6, [Inv dec, sc 11] 3 times, Inv dec, sc 5. {48}

Round 31: sc around. {48}

Round 32: sc 6, [Inv dec, sc 10] 3 times, Inv dec, sc 4. {44}

Round 33: sc around. {44}

Round 34: sc 6, [Inv dec, sc 9] 3 times, Inv dec, sc 3. {40}

Round 35: sc around. {40}

Round 36: sc 6, [Inv dec, sc 8] 3 times, Inv dec, sc 2. {36}

Round 37: sc around. {36}

Round 38: [sc 4, Inv dec] around. {30}

Stuff the body firmly with polyester fiberfill.

Round 39: sc around. {30}

Round 40: sc 2, [Inv dec, sc 3] 5 times, inv dec, sc. {24}

Round 41: [sc 2, Inv dec] around. {18}

Round 42: [Inv dec, sc] around. {12}

Round 43: [Inv dec] around. {6}

Fasten and leave a long tail for sewing.

Head

With Yellow yarn:

Round 1: sc 6 in magic ring. {6}

Round 2: [inc] around. {12}

Round 3: [inc, sc] around. {18}

Round 4: [sc 2. inc] around. {24}

Round 5: [inc, sc 3] around. {30}

Round 6: sc 2, [inc, sc 4] 5 times, inc, sc 2. {36}

Round 7: [inc, sc 5] around. {42}

Round 8: sc around. {42}

Round 9: sc 3, [inc, sc 6] 5 times, inc, sc 3. {48}

Round 10: sc around. {48}

Round 11: [inc, sc 7] around. {54}

Round 12 - 13: sc around. {54}

Round 14: sc 4, [inc, sc 8] 5 times, inc, sc 4. {60}

Round 15 - 16: sc around. {60}

Round 17: [inc, sc 9] around. {66}

Round 18 - 24: sc around. {66}

Round 25: [inv dec, sc 9] around. {60}

Round 26: sc around. {60}

Round 27: sc 4, [inv dec, sc 8] 5 times, inv dec, sc 4. {54}

Round 28: sc around. {54}

Round 29: [inv dec, sc 7] around. {48}

Round 30: sc 3, [inv dec, sc 6] 5 times, inv dec, sc 3. {42}

Round 31: [inv dec, sc 5] around. {36}

Round 32: sc 2, [inv dec, sc 4] 5 times, inv dec, sc 2. {30}

Round 33: [inv dec, sc 3] around. {24}

Stuff with polyester fillings, sew muzzle. Remove stuffing to install safety nose. Re-stuff again and continue to complete the head.

Round 34: sc, [inv dec, sc 2] 5 times, inv dec, sc. {18}

Round 35: [inv dec, sc 1] around. {12}

Round 36: [inv dec] around. {6}

Fasten and hide yarn end.

#

Muzzle

Make 2 with Beige yarn:

Round 1: sc 6 in magic ring. {6}

Round 2: [inc] around. {12}

Round 3: [inc, sc] around. {18}

Round 4: [sc 2. inc] around. {24}

Round 5: [inc, sc 3] around. {30}

Fasten and leave a long tail for sewing.

Sew 2 circles alongside together (about 4 stitches) to form the muzzle.

#

Ears

Make 2 with Yellow yarn:

Round 1: Sc 4 in magic ring. {4}

Round 2: sc around. {4}

Round 3: [inc] around. {8}

Round 4: sc around. {8}

Round 5: [inc, sc] around. {12}

Round 6: [inc, sc 2] around. {16}

Round 7: [inc, sc 3] around. {20}

Round 8: sc around. {20}

Round 9: [inc, sc 4] around. {24}

Round 10 - 15: sc around {24}

Fasten and leave a long tail for sewing.

Fold the ear and sew the bottom to give it a scooped appearance.

#

Arms

Make 2 starting with Light Khaki yarn:

Round 1: sc 6 in magic ring. {6}

Round 2: [inc] around. {12}

Round 3: [inc, sc] around. {18}

Round 4: [sc 2. inc] around. {24}

Round 5: [inc, sc 3] around. {30}

Change yarn color to Yellow.

Round 6 – 10: sc around. {30}

Round 11: [sc 8, Inv dec] around. {27}

Round 12 - 13: sc around. {27}

Round 14: [sc 7, Inv dec] around. {24}

Round 15 – 16: sc around. {24}

Round 17: [sc 6, Inv dec] around. {21}

Round 18 – 19: sc around. {21}

Round 20: [sc 5, Inv dec] around. {18}

Round 21 – 22: sc around {18}.

Round 23: [sc 4, Inv dec] around. {15}

Round 24 – 35: sc around. {15}

Fasten and leave a long tail for sewing.

Fill the bottom 2/3 of the arms firmly with polyester fiberfill.

#

Animals Amigurumi

Legs

Make 2 starting with Light Khaki yarn:

Round 1: ch5, Inc in 2nd ch from hook, sc 2, 5sc in the last ch. Continue on the other side of the chain base, sc 2, 3sc in the last ch. {14}

Round 2: Inc, sc 4, [Inc] 3 times, sc 4, [Inc] 2 times. {20}

Round 3: Inc, sc 6, [Inc] 2 times, sc, Inc, sc 6, [Inc] 2 times, sc. {26}

Round 4: Inc, sc 8, [Inc, sc] 2 times, Inc, sc 8, [Inc, sc] 2 times. {32}

Round 5: Inc, sc 10, Inc, sc 2, Inc, sc, Inc, sc 10, Inc, sc 2, Inc, sc. {38}

Round 6: Inc. sc 12, [Inc, sc 2] 2 times, Inc, sc 12, [Inc, sc 2] 2 times. {44}

Change yarn color to Yellow.

Round 7 – 10: sc around. {44}

Round 11: sc 14, Inv dec, sc 12, Inv dec, sc 14. {42}

Round 12: sc 14, Inv dec, sc 10, Inv dec, sc 14. {40}

Round 13: sc 14, Inv dec, sc 8, Inv dec, sc 14. {38}

Round 14: sc 14, Inv dec, sc 6, Inv dec, sc 14. {36}

Round 15: sc 14, Inv dec, sc 4, Inv dec, sc 14. {34}

Round 16: sc 14, Inv dec, sc 2, Inv dec, sc 14. {32}

Round 17: sc 14, Inv dec, Inv dec, sc 14. {30}

Round 18: sc around. {30}

Round 19: [sc 6, Inv dec] 3 times, sc 6. {27}

Round 20 – 21: sc around. {27}

Round 22: sc 6, [Inv dec, sc 5] 3 times. {24}

Round 23 – 24: sc around. {24}

Round 25: sc 5, Inv dec, sc 10, Inv dec, sc 5. {22}

Round 26 – 27: sc around. {22}

Round 28: sc 5, Inv dec, sc 9, Inv dec, sc 4. {20}

Round 29 – 30: sc around. {20}

Round 31: sc 4, Inv dec, sc 8, Inv dec, sc 4. {18}

Fasten and leave a long tail for sewing.

Fill the bottom 2/3 of the legs firmly with polyester fiberfill.

#

Tail

With Yellow yarn:

ch 4, slst to form a ring.

ch1, sc 4 into the ring. sc around until the tail is 4" long, slst.

Change yarn color to Light Khaki.

ch3, ps3 in each st, slst. Hide both Yellow and Light Khaki yarn end into the tail.

ch, Inv dec around, slst, ch

Fasten off. Trim near the knot. Apply tiny craft glue to the end and shape it pointy.

\#

More Details on how to crochet Leon, the Lion Amigurumi

After completed round 33 of the Head part, stuff the head to polyester filling.
Pin the muzzle to the head, with the center of the muzzle at 2nd round of the Head.
Sew around the muzzle, stuff some polyester filling to the muzzle before finish up.

Animals Amigurumi

Sew a philtrum line with black yarn.

Remove polyester filling to install safety nose through the starting hole of the head.

Re-stuff the head again after the safety nose has been installed. Crochet to complete the head.

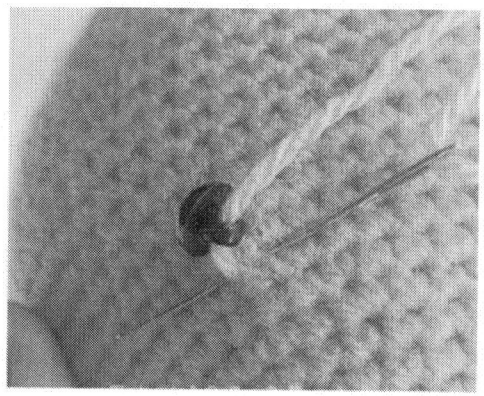

Sew eyes at round 13, 17 stitches apart.
Do not cut the yarn after sewing the first eye, instead, insert it into the head and come out from the second eye to sew another eye.

Pull the yarn a little to sink the eyes a little to the head, knot securely. You can run the yarn through the head a few times to prevent the yarn from snapping in the long run.

Sew the ears to the head, about 6 rounds at the back of the eyes. The contact area between the base of the ear and head is a form of triangle shape.

Crochet and get ready the rest of the parts for final assembly.

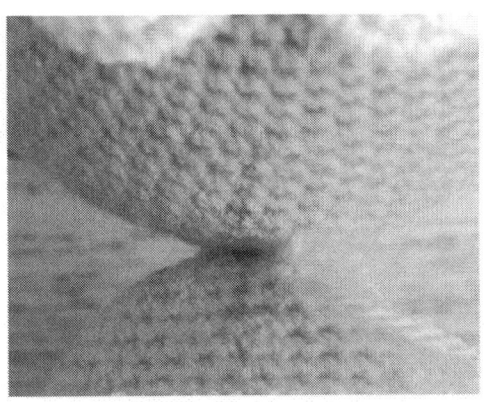

Mark the centerline below the head and the top of the body. Position the head to the body (refer the picture) below. Sew the head to the body at 1 stitch away from the centerlines, sew about 7 stitches from center of the body to the front, followed by 2 stitches to the side. Sew about 9 stitches to the back and another 2 stitches to the side followed by 2 stitches to complete the stitching.

The contact area of the head is a rectangle of 9 sts x 2 sts.

The head will tilt a little to the front.

Sew arms at the side, next to the seam of the head and body.

Followed by sewing legs at round 15 (from the bottom) of the body.

Lastly, sew the tail to the back of the body

Sew 3 black lines on each limb as the toe lines of the lion.

Animals Amigurumi

The front of the lion amigurumi.

Without a mane, Leon, the lion amigurumi doesn't look happy.

The back of the lion amigurumi.

Wind yarn around the 4" cardboard, the lion needs about 1000 of 4" strips to be tied on the head.

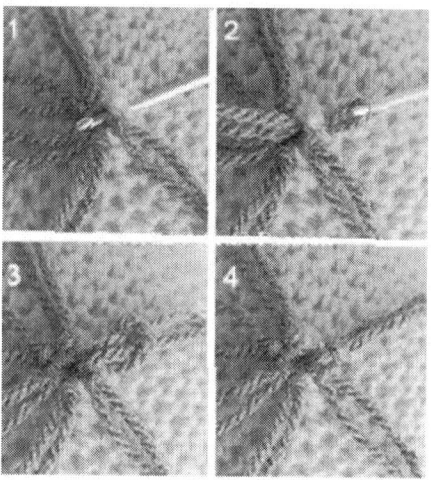

Starting from the back of the head, fasten the yarn strip as shown in the picture.

Fasten to mane in every stitch to have a full and fluffy hair for the lion.

After a few rounds, the pile starts to show fuller.

It takes time to fasten, please be a little patience.

Continue to fasten until 2 rounds away from the eyes; 4 rounds after the ear.

Fasten more at the chin of the lion by following the shape of the muzzle at at distance of about 4 stitches away.

It takes about a day to fasten the mane but the outcome is flattering. The soft and fluffiness of the mane is such a cozy little softie to hug and cuddle.

As the King of the jungle, Leon is looking over his land to make sure everything is fine.

Animals Amigurumi

SOCK MONKEY AMIGURUMI CROCHET PATTERN

Materials

- Yarn in white, melon red, pistachio green and pastel blue (I used Lion Brand's BabySoft Acrylic Yarn)
- Embroidery Floss in Yellow
- 2 x 11.5mm black buttons or safety eyes
- White felt

Tools

- 2.5mm hook
- white sewing thread and sewing needle
- Tapestry needle

- Polyester fiberfill

Instructions

Abbreviations

Ch: chain

Sc: single crochet

Inc: sc2 in a stitch

Inv dec: invisible decrease

slst: slip stitch

sk: skip

Amigurumi Crochet pattern

(all pattern works in spiral round except muzzle)

Head and Body

Working top down.

Start with red yarn

Slip knot, Ch 2.

Round 1: Sc 6 in the second chain from the hook {6}.

Round 2: [Inc] around {12}.

Round 3: [Inc, sc in next st] around {18}.

Round 4: [Inc, sc in next 2 st] around {24}.

Round 5: [Inc, sc in next 3 st] around {30}.

Round 6: [Inc, sc in next 4 st] around {36}.

Round 7: [Inc, sc in next 5 st] around {42}.

Round 8: [Inc, sc in next 6 st] around {48}.

Round 9: [Inc, sc in next 7 st] around {54}.

Round 10: [Inc, sc in next 8 st] around {60}.

Round 11-22: Sc around {60}.

Change yarn to white (read Note below for jog-less join for stripes)

Round 23-30: Sc around {60}.

Change yarn to green

Round 31-36: Sc around {60}.

Round 37: [Inv dec, sc in next 8 st] around {54}.

Round 38: [Inv dec, sc in next 7 st] around {48}.

Change yarn to white

Round 39: Sc around {48}.

Round 40: [Inc, sc in next 7 st] around {54}.

Round 41: [Inc, sc in next 8 st] around {60}.

Round 42-46: Sc around {60}.

Change yarn to blue

Round 47-54: Sc around {60}.

Change yarn to white

Round 55-62: Sc around {60}.

Change yarn to red

Round 63-70: Sc around {60}.

Shaped hip (to create a bottom while make an opening to accommodate the legs)

Round 71: sc in next 18 st, ch 18, sk 30 st, sc in next 12 st {48}.

Round 72: Sc around {48}.

Round 73: [Inv dec, sc in next 6 st] around {42}.

Round 74: [Inv dec, sc in next 5 st] around {36}.

Round 75: [Inv dec, sc in next 4 st] around {30}.

Round 76: [Inv dec, sc in next 3 st] around {24}.

Round 77: [Inv dec, sc in next 2 st] around {18}.

Round 78: [Inv dec, sc in next st] around {12}.

Round 79: Inv dec around {6}.

Fasten off and hide yarn.

Stuff head and body.

Legs

Mark the center lines of the hip to make 2 parts for the left and right legs respectively (refer the tutorial picture). Count from the side of the body at the opening, 15 sts on the body and 9 sts on the hip.

Left leg

Start with white yarn

Round 1: Slip knot, ch5, sc in next 15 st on the body side (at the marking), sc in the corner between the hip and the body, sc in next 9 st on the hip side {30}.

Round 2-8: sc around {30}.

Change yarn to green

Round 9-16: sc around {30}.

Change yarn to white

Round 17-24: sc around {30}.

Change yarn to blue

Round 25-32: sc around {30}.

Change yarn to white

Round 33-40: sc around {30}.

Change yarn to red

Round 41-48: sc around {30}.

Change yarn to white

Round 49-56: sc around {30}.

Change yarn to green

Round 57-66: sc around {30}.

Round 67: [Inv dec, sc in next 4 st] around {25}.

Round 68: [Inv dec, sc in next 3 st] around {20}.

Stuff

Round 69: [Inv dec, sc in next 2 st] around {15}.

Round 70: [Inv dec, sc in next st] around {10}.

Round 71: Inv dec around {5}.

Fasten off and leave a long tail for sewing.

Animals Amigurumi

Right leg

Start with white yarn

Slip knot, ch 5.

Round 1: sc in next 9 st on the hip side (at the marking), sc in the corner between the hip and the body, sc in next 15 st on the body side {30}.

Round 2-71: follow the left leg pattern.

Fasten off and hide yarn.

Muzzle

Use red yarn.

Slip knot, ch 13.

Round 1: sc in second ch from hook, sc in next 10 st, 4sc in next st (aka first ch st), turn around (not flip) and work on the other loops of the chain stitch, sc in next 10 st, 3sc in next st, slst to the beginning st to form a round {28}.

Round 2: ch1, *sc in next 12 st, 2sc in next 2 st, repeat * 2 times, slst {32}.

Round 3: ch1, *sc in next 12 st, 2sc in next st, sc in next 2 st, 2sc in next st, * 2 times, slst {36}.

Round 4: ch1, *sc in next 12 st, 2sc in next st, sc in next 4 st, 2sc in next st, repeat * 2 times, slst {40}.

Round 5: ch1, *sc in next 12 st, 2sc in next st, sc in next 6 st, 2sc in next st, repeat * 2 times, slst {44}.

Round 6: ch1, *sc in next 12 st, 2sc in next st, sc in next 8 st, 2sc in next st, repeat * 2 times, slst {48}.

Round 7: ch1, *sc in next 12 st, 2sc in next st, sc in next 10 st, 2sc in next st, repeat * 2 times, slst {52}.

Round 8: ch1, *sc in next 12 st, 2sc in next st, sc in next 12 st, 2sc in next st, repeat * 2 times, slst {56}.

Round 9-13: sc around {56}.

Fasten off and leave a long tail for sewing.

Sew a brunch stitch line across the center with yellow embroidery floss.

Note that the ch stitch at the beginning of the round and the slst stitch at the end of the round are just transition stitches, please do not count them into the total stitches in the round nor crochet any stitches on them.

Ears

Make 2.

Start with red or green yarn

Slip knot, ch2.

Round 1: Sc 5 in the second ch from hook {5}.

Round 2: [Inc] around {10}.

Round 3: [Inc, sc in next st] around {15}.

Round 4: [Inc, sc in next 2 st] around {20}.

Round 5: [Inc, sc in next 3 st] around {25}.

Round 6-8: Sc around {25}.

Change yarn to white

Round 9: sc in next st, [Inv dec, sc in next 6 st] around {22}.

Round 10: sc in next st, [Inv dec, sc in next 5 st] around {19}.

Round 11: sc in next st, [Inv dec, sc in next 4 st] around {16}.

Round 12: sc around {16}.

Fasten off and leave a long tail for sewing.

Arms

Make 2.

Animals Amigurumi

Start with green yarn

Slip knot, ch2.

Round 1: Sc 5 in the second ch from hook {5}.

Round 2: [Inc] around {10}.

Round 3: [Inc, sc in next st] around {15}.

Round 4: [Inc, sc in next 2 st] around {20}.

Round 5: [Inc, sc in next 3 st] around {25}.

Round 6-15: Sc around {25}.

Change yarn to white

Round 16-23: Sc around {25}.

Change yarn to red

Round 24-31: Sc around {25}.

Change yarn to white

Round 32-39: Sc around {25}.

Change yarn to blue

Round 40-47: Sc around {25}.

Change yarn to white

Round 48-55: Sc around {25}.

Change yarn to green

Round 56-63: Sc around {25}.

Change yarn to white

Round 64-69: Sc around {25}.

Stuff

Round 70: [Inv dec, sc in next 3 st] around {20}.

Round 71: [Inv dec, sc in next 2 st] around {15}.

Round 72: [Inv dec, sc in next st] around {10}.

Fasten off and leave a long tail for sewing.

Tail

Start with green yarn

Slip knot, ch2.

Round 1: Sc 5 in the second ch from hook {5}.

Round 2: [Inc] around {10}.

Round 3-15: Sc around {10}.

Change yarn to white

Round 16-23: Sc around {10}.

Change yarn to red

Round 24-31: Sc around {10}.

Change yarn to white

Round 32-39: Sc around {10}.

Change yarn to blue

Round 40-47: Sc around {10}.

Change yarn to white

Round 48-55: Sc around {10}.

Change yarn to green

Round 56-63: Sc around {10}.

Change yarn to white

Round 64-71: Sc around {10}.

Change yarn to red

Round 72-79: Sc around {10}.

Change yarn to white

Round 80-87: Sc around {10}.

Change yarn to blue

Round 88-95: Sc around {10}.

Change yarn to white

Round 96-103: Sc around {10}.

Change yarn to green

Round 104-111: Sc around {10}.

Change yarn to white

Round 112-119: Sc around {10}.

Fasten off and leave a long tail for sewing.

Assembly

1. Sew to close all openings of the parts with a tapestry needle.

2. Cut white of eye from white felt. Sew black button to the felt. Decorate the eyes with yellow running stitch near the edge. Sew eyes to the face with white thread.

3. Mark the muzzle on the face with an erasable fabric marker. The shape is rounded corner rectangular. Sew muzzle to the face, stuff before finish-off the sewing.

4. Sew on the arms, ears, and tail.

Animals Amigurumi

Notes

1. For jogless color change (near to perfect straight join) for stripes, please read this tutorial (video included).

2. This monkey amigurumi pattern is developed based on the sock monkey I sewed, the position of the body parts are the same, if you need to have a closer look on the detail, please refer to the sock monkey tutorial.

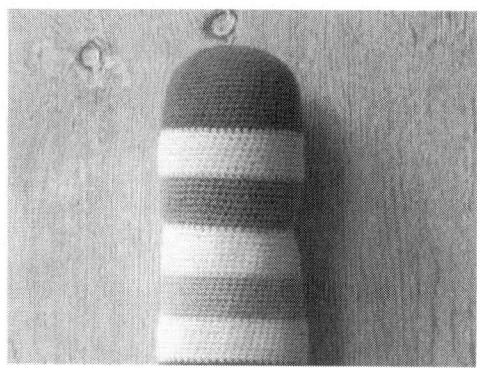

This is the body with the hip part and an opening for the legs.

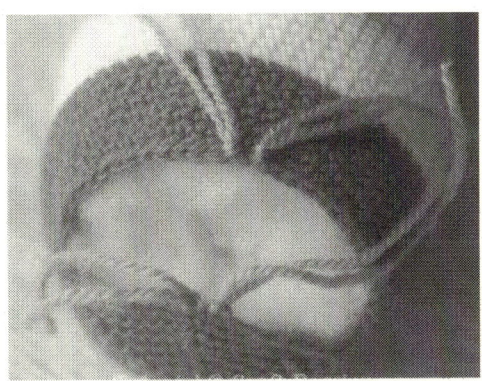

This are the markings to separate the hip in 2 parts for the legs.

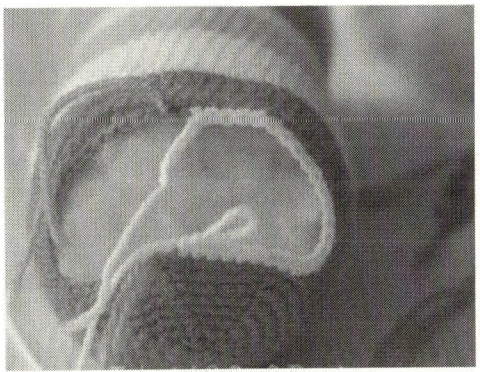

Take off the marking of the left legs and crochet as per pattern instruction. Note that the left leg starts from the front part of the hip.

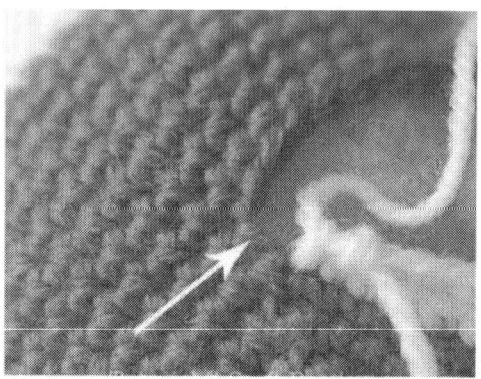

This is where you need to crochet an extra stitch at the corner of the hip, it is indeed the side of an sc stitch.

Continue crochet in the spiral round to build the left leg.

Animals Amigurumi

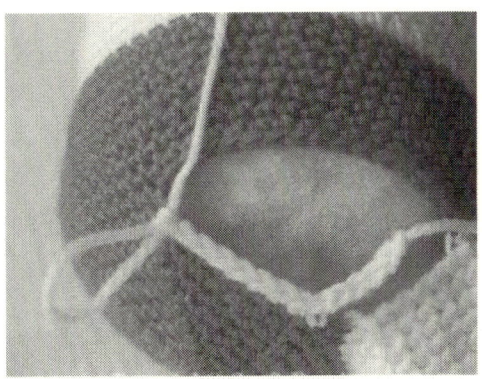

This is the right leg. Note the pattern instruction, the first 5 chains is a pre-round 1 base.
Follow the instruction to crochet and not forgetting the extra stitch you need to make at the corner.

The round complete after you have crochet on the 5 chains of the pre-round 1.

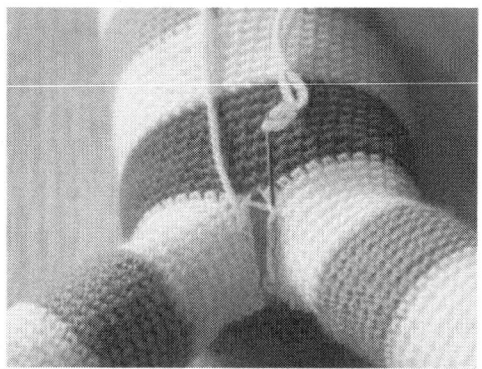

Sew up the opening between the legs after you have completed the stuffing.

In order for the monkey to be able to sit on its own, don't stuff too much between the hips and legs.

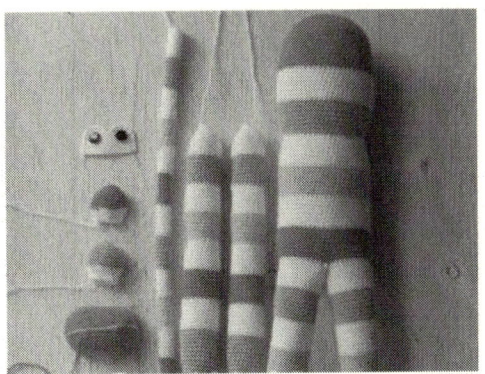

Complete the rest of the parts according to the amigurumi pattern.

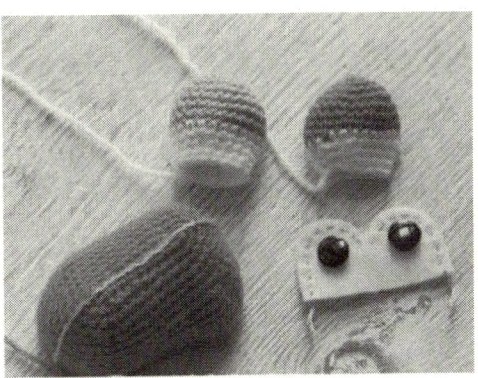

A closer look on the muzzle, eyes, and ears; especially the details on the yellow embroidery lines.

Sew eyes on the face and mark the muzzle position with an erasable fabric marker. The muzzle marking shape is rounded corner rectangular.

Pin the muzzle to the face so that it is aligned. Sew it on and stuff before finished off the sewing.

Stuff a small bit of polyester fiberfill to the ears, sew up the opening.

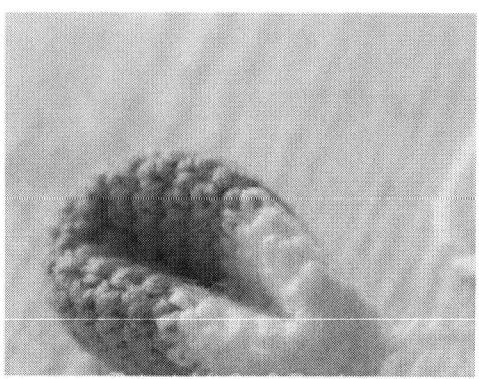

Bend the ear and sew to make a cup-like ear. Sew them on the side of the face.

Sew to close the opening of the arms. Sew them on the side of the body.

Animals Amigurumi

Here are the twin brothers monkey, the sock monkey (left) and the amigurumi monkey. Aren't they look alike even though they are not identical twins (one sewed from socks and one crochet from yarn).

FOX AMIGURUMI PATTERN

Animals Amigurumi

Fox Amigurumi Pattern

Mr. Furu

Height: 10" tall

Skill level: Intermediate

Duration: About 8 hours

Abbreviations

Crochet (in US Terms)

ch: chain

sc: single crochet

ssc = split single crochet / knit stitch / waistcoat stitch

Inc: 2ssc increase

Dec: ssc 2 stitches together

Others

R: Round

OR: Orange Yarn

Animals Amigurumi

BL: Black Yarn

WH: White Yarn

Materials

1. 3.5mm hook

2. Acrylic yarn (50 gram each ball): white (1 ball), black (1 ball) and orange (2 balls)

3. Colored Iris Safety Eyes, Brown, 10mm size, 2

4. Safety Nose, 18mm size, 1

5. Doll Wired Glasses (optional)

6. Darning needle

7. Polyester fiberfill

8. Scissors

9. Pins

Important Note: This is a colorwork amigurumi using Split Single Crochet / Knit Stitch / Waistcoat Stitch method. Please DO NOT attempt to convert it to normal Single Crochet.

Animals Amigurumi

Why use Split Sing Crochet instead of normal Single Crochet?

Please take note that this amigurumi pattern is using Split Single Crochet (SSC), some may know it as Crochet Knit Stitch or Waistcoat Stitch. Unlike the normal Single Crochet, SSC inserts hook in between the legs of the next st. In colorwork amigurumi where stitches are crochet in the continuous round, SSC keeps the colorwork vertically straight throughout the round. It is because the hook is inserted in between the legs of next stitch, but if you are using normal Single Crochet, the colorwork will lean to the right or left depending if you are right handed or left handed.

How to change yarn color in colorwork crochet?

Follow the pattern to work on stitches in color A until the last yarn over, pull through the loop with the new color B. Leave the color A behind until it is time to work on it again. Continue to work in Color B until it is time to change the color back to A, on the last stitch in the color B, just pull through the color A on the last yarn over and drop the color B. Leave a decent length of the unwork yarn between the color change so that it won't distort the shape of your amigurumi. Repeat this until you have completed the pattern.

Note: I don't hide the unworked yarn between the stitches because it will cause distortion in stitch height, especially in SSC stitch.

Fox Amigurumi Crochet Pattern

Head

With Orange yarn:

R1: sc 4 in a magic ring {4}

R2: [Inc] 4 times. {8}

R3: [Inc, ssc] 4 times. {12}

R4: [ssc 2, Inc] 4 times. {16}

R5: ssc, [Inc, ssc 3] 3 times, Inc, ssc 2. {20}

R6: ssc 3, [Inc, ssc 4] 3 times, Inc, ssc. {24}

R7: [ssc 5, Inc] 4 times. {28}

R8: [Inc, ssc6] 4 times. {32}

R9: ssc 2, [Inc, ssc 7] 3 times, Inc, ssc 5. {36}

R10: ssc 4, [Inc, ssc 8] 3 times, Inc, ssc 4. {40}

R11: ssc 6, [Inc, ssc 9] 3 times, Inc, ssc 3. {44}

R12: ssc 8, [Inc, ssc 10] 3 times, Inc, ssc 2 {48}

R13 – R17: ssc around. {48}

Colorwork begins here (OR – Orange, WH – White)

R18: OR [ssc 15], WH [ssc 3], OR [ssc 12], WH [ssc 3], OR [ssc 15]. {48}

R19: OR [ssc 15], WH [ssc 4], OR [ssc 10], WH [ssc 4], OR [ssc 15]. {48}

R20: OR [ssc 14], WH [ssc 6], OR [ssc 8], WH [ssc 6], OR [ssc 14]. {48}

R21: OR [ssc 14], WH [ssc 7], OR [ssc 6], WH [ssc 7], OR [ssc 14]. {48}

R22: OR [ssc 13], WH [ssc 9], OR [ssc 4], WH [ssc 9], OR [ssc 13]. {48}

R23 – 27: OR [ssc 13], WH [ssc 22], OR [ssc 13]. {48}

R28: OR [ssc 13], WH [ssc 35]. {48}

Change to White yarn only:

R29: [Dec, ssc 10] 4 times {44}

R30: ssc 4, [Dec, ssc 9] 3 times, Dec, ssc 5. {40}

R31: [ssc 8, Dec] 4 times. {36}

R32: ssc 2, [Dec, ssc 4] 5 times, Dec, ssc 2. {30}

R33: [Dec, ssc 3] 6 times. {24}

R34: [ssc 2, Dec] 6 times. {18}

Install safety eyes, neaten stranded yarns if needed (refer Pic 1 and 2)

Stuff

R35: [ssc, Dec] 6 times. {12}

R36: [Dec] 6 times. {6}

Fasten off and leave a long tail for sewing.

Muzzle

With White yarn

R1: sc 4 in a magic ring {4}

R2: Inc, ssc 2, Inc. {6}

R3: Inc 2 times, ssc, 1 ch (skip 1 st), ssc, Inc. {9}

Colorwork begins here (OR – Orange, WH – White)

R4: WH [ssc 3, Inc], OR [ssc 3], WH [Inc 2 times]. {12}

R5: WH [ssc 3, Inc, ssc], OR [ssc 3], WH [ssc, Inc] 2 times. {15}

R6: WH [Inc, ssc 3, Inc], OR [ssc 5], WH [ssc, Inc, ssc 3]. {18}

R7: WH [Inc, ssc 4, Inc, ssc], OR [ssc 5], WH [ssc, Inc, ssc 4]. {21}

R8 – R9: WH [ssc 9], OR [ssc 5], WH [ssc 7]. {21}

Fasten off and leave a long tail for sewing.

Install safety nose through the ch st at R3.

Ear, make 2

With Black yarn:

R1: sc 3 in a magic ring {3}

R2: [Inc] 3 times. {6}

Colorwork begins here (BL – Black, OR – Orange, WH – White)

R3: BL [Inc, ssc], WH [Inc], BL [ssc, Inc, ssc]. {9}

R4: BL [ssc, Inc, ssc], WH [ssc, Inc], BL [ssc 2, Inc, ssc]. {12}

R5: BL [ssc, Inc, ssc 2], WH [ssc, Inc, ssc], BL [ssc 2, Inc, ssc 2]. {15}

R6: BL [ssc 5], WH [ssc 4], BL [ssc 6]. {15}

R7 – R10: OR [ssc 5], WH [ssc 4], OR [ssc 6]. {15}

Fasten off and leave a long tail for sewing.

Body

With Orange yarn:

R1: sc 6 in a magic ring {6}

R2: [Inc] 6 times. {12}

R3: [ssc 2, Inc] 4 times. {16}

R4: ssc, [Inc, ssc 3] 3 times, Inc, ssc 2. {20}

R5: ssc 3, [Inc, ssc 4] 3 times, Inc, ssc. {24}

R6: [ssc 5, Inc] 4 times. {28}

R7: [Inc, ssc6] 4 times. {32}

R8: ssc 2, [Inc, ssc 7] 3 times, Inc, ssc 5. {36}

R9: ssc 4, [Inc, ssc 8] 3 times, Inc, ssc 4. {40}

R10: ssc 6, [Inc, ssc 9] 3 times, Inc, ssc 3. {44}

R11 – R15: ssc around. {44}

Colorwork begins here (OR – Orange, WH – White)

R16: OR [ssc 21], WH [ssc], OR [ssc 22]. {44}

R17: OR [ssc 10, Dec, ssc 8], WH [ssc 3], OR [ssc 8, Dec, ssc 11].

{42}

R18: OR [ssc 6, Dec, ssc 10], WH [ssc 5], OR [ssc 10, Dec, ssc 7].

{40}

R19: OR [ssc 13, Dec, ssc 2], WH [ssc 5], OR [ssc 2, Dec, ssc 14].

{38}

R20: OR [ssc 3, Dec, ssc 10], WH [ssc 7], OR [ssc 10, Dec, ssc 4].

{36}

R21: OR [ssc 6, Dec, ssc 6], WH [ssc 7], OR [ssc 6, Dec, ssc 7]. {34}

R22: OR [ssc 10, Dec, ssc 1], WH [ssc 7], OR [ssc 1, Dec, ssc 11].

{32}

R23: OR [ssc 2, Dec, ssc 7], WH [ssc 9], OR [ssc 7, Dec, ssc 3]. {30}

R24: OR [ssc 7], WH [ssc], OR [ssc 2], WH [ssc 3, Dec, ssc 4], OR [ssc 2], WH [ssc], OR [ssc 6, Dec]. {28}

R25: OR [ssc 3, Dec, ssc], WH [ssc 3], OR [ssc], WH [ssc 8], OR [ssc], WH [ssc 3], OR [ssc, Dec, ssc 3]. {26}

R26: OR [ssc, Dec, ssc 2], WH [ssc 3], OR [ssc], WH [ssc 8], OR [ssc], WH [ssc 3], OR [ssc 2, Dec, ssc]. {24}

R27: OR [ssc 3], WH [ssc 3, Dec, 8, Dec, ssc 3], OR [ssc 3]. {22}

R28: OR [Dec, ssc], WH [ssc 7, Dec, ssc 7], OR [ssc 3]. {20}

R29: OR [ssc], WH [ssc 2, Dec, 9, Dec, ssc 2], OR [ssc 2]. {18}

Neaten stranded yarns if needed

Stuff

Change to White yarn only:

R30: ssc 5, Dec, ssc 3, Dec, ssc 6. {16}

R31: [ssc 6, Dec] 2 times. {14}

R32: ssc 2, Dec, ssc 6, Dec, ssc 2. {12}

R33: [Dec] 6 times. {6}

Fasten off and leave a long tail for sewing.

Arm, make 2

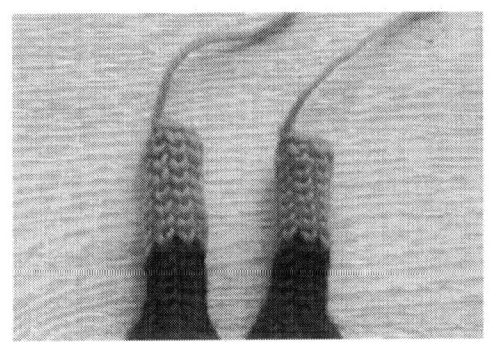

With Black yarn:

R1: sc 4 in a magic ring {4}

R2: [Inc] 4 times. {8}

R3: [Inc, ssc] 4 times. {12}

R4: [ssc 2, Inc] 4 times. {16}

R5 – R6 : ssc around {16}

R7: [Dec, ssc 2] 4 times. {12}

R8: [ssc, Dec] 4 times. {8}

R9 – R14: ssc around. {8}

Change to Orange yarn only:

R15 – R22: ssc around. {8}

Fasten off and leave a long tail for sewing.

Stuff

Leg, make 2

With Black yarn:

R1: sc 6 in a magic ring {6}

R2: [Inc] 6 times. {12}

R3: [ssc 2, Inc] 4 times. {16}

R4: ssc, [Inc, ssc 3] 3 times, Inc, ssc 2. {20}

R5 – R7: ssc around. {20}

R8: ssc, [Dec, ssc 3] 3 times, Dec, ssc 2. {16}

R9: [ssc 2, Dec] 4 times. {12}

R10 – R13: ssc around. {12}

Change to Orange yarn only:

R14 – R17: ssc around. {12}

Fasten off and leave a long tail for sewing.

Stuff

Tail

With White yarn:

R1: sc 3 in a magic ring {3}

R2: [Inc] 3 times. {6}

R3: ssc around. {6}

R4: [Inc, ssc] 3 times. {9}

R5: [ssc 2, Inc] 3 times. {12}

R6: ssc, [Inc, ssc 3] 2 times, Inc, ssc 2. {15}

R7: ssc 3, [Inc, ssc 4] 2 times, Inc, ssc. {18}

R8: [ssc 5, Inc] 3 times. {21}

R9: [Inc, ssc6] 3 times. {24}

Colorwork begins here (OR – Orange, WH – White)

R10: WH [ssc 3], OR [ssc], WH [ssc 7], OR [ssc], WH [ssc 3], OR [ssc], WH [ssc 7], OR [ssc]. {24}

R11: OR [ssc], WH [ssc], OR [ssc 3], WH [ssc 5], OR [ssc 3], WH [ssc], OR [ssc 3], WH [ssc 5], OR [ssc 2]. {24}

R12: OR [ssc 6], WH [ssc 3], OR [ssc 9], WH [ssc 3], OR [ssc 3]. {24}

R13: OR [ssc 7], WH [ssc], OR [ssc 11], WH [ssc], OR [ssc 4]. {24}

Change to Orange yarn only:

R14 – R20: ssc around. {24}

R21: [Dec, ssc 6] 3 times. {21}

R22: ssc around. {21}

R23: ssc 2, [Dec, ssc 5] 2 times, Dec, ssc 3. {18}

R24: ssc around. {18}

R25: [ssc 4, Dec] 3 times. {15}

R26: ssc around. {15}

Stuff

R27: [Dec, ssc 3] 3 times. {12}

R28: ssc around. {12}

R29: [ssc 2, Dec] 3 times. {9}

R30: ssc around. {9}

R31: [Dec, ssc], 3 times. {6}

R32: ssc around. {6}

Fasten off and leave a long tail for sewing.

Fox Amigurumi Assembly

Pic 1

This is how the inside of the colorwork amigurumi looks. You may leave the unworked yarn stranded as it is. If you have left a decent length of yarn between the colorwork, then you are fine to leave them as it is. If the yarns are too short, you may trim the yarn and knot them together as shown in Pic 2.

Pic 2

Personally, I prefer to neaten my lengthy unworked yarn stranded across the colorwork section. The clean interior is easier for stuffing and shaping.

Align the muzzle of the fox amigurumi with the marking between the eyes as shown in the picture. Pin, sew and stuff the muzzle to the head.

Next, position and pin the ears to the head. Make sure bother ears are aligned and in symmetry.

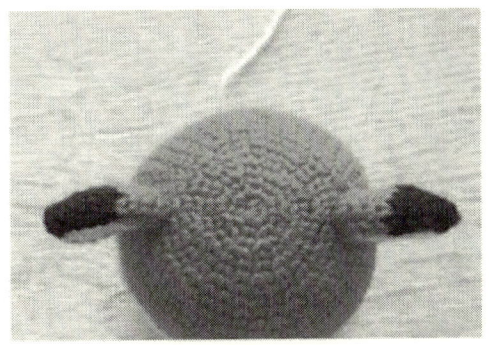

This is the top view of the head of the fox amigurumi. A better view of the locations of the ears.

Position all parts together. First, sew the head to the body, followed by the arms, legs, and tail respectively.

Mr. Furu, the Fox Amigurumi is done, put on his glasses and he is ready to go all out to the woodland.

You may sew the tail pointing upwards instead of pointing downward.

RACCOON AMIGURUMI PATTERN

Amigurumi Pattern

Jr. **Rakku**

Height: 10" tall

Skill level: Intermediate

Duration: About 8 hours

Description:

Jr. Rakku, the Raccoon Amigurumi is rather different from the general character of his own kind, he is young, gentle and innocent, he trusts everything that others told him. Perhaps **Mr. Furu** could teach him a little old fox trick to make him smarter to survive in the woodland.

Abbreviations

Crochet (in US Terms)

ch: chain

sc: single crochet

ssc = split single crochet / knit stitch / waistcoat stitch

Inc: 2ssc increase

Dec: ssc 2 stitches together

slst: slip stitch

Others

R: Round

GR: Gray Yarn

BL: Black Yarn

WH: White Yarn

Materials

1. 3.5mm hook

2. Acrylic yarn (50 gram each ball): white (1 ball), black (1 ball) and

Animals Amigurumi

gray (1 ball)

3. Colored Iris Safety Eyes, Gray, 10mm size, 2

4. Safety Nose, 18mm size, 1

5. Felt, White, 1.5" x 1.5", cut into 2 pcs. of 1/2" circles

6. Doll Wired Glasses (optional)

7. Darning needle

8. Polyester fiberfill

9. Scissors

10. Pins

Important Note: This is a colorwork amigurumi using Split Single Crochet / Knit Stitch / Waistcoat Stitch method. Please DO NOT attempt to convert it to normal Single Crochet.

<u>Why use Split Sing Crochet instead of normal Single Crochet?</u>
Please take note that this amigurumi pattern is using <u>Split Single Crochet (SSC)</u>, some may know it as Crochet Knit Stitch or Waistcoat Stitch. Unlike the normal Single Crochet, SSC inserts hook in between the legs of the next st. In colorwork amigurumi where stitches are crochet in the continuous round, SSC keeps the colorwork vertically straight throughout the round. It is because the

hook is inserted in between the legs of next stitch, but if you are using normal Single Crochet, the colorwork will lean to the right or left depending if you are right handed or left handed.

How to change yarn color in colorwork crochet?
Follow the pattern to work on stitches in color A until the last yarn over, pull through the loop with the new color B. Leave the color A behind until it is time to work on it again. Continue to work in Color B until it is time to change the color back to A, on the last stitch in the color B, just pull through the color A on the last yarn over and drop the color B. Leave a decent length of the unwork yarn between the color change so that it won't distort the shape of your amigurumi. Repeat this until you have completed the pattern.

Note: I don't hide the unworked yarn between the stitches because it will cause distortion in stitch height, especially in SSC stitch.

Raccoon Amigurumi: Crochet Pattern

Head

With Gray yarn:

R1: sc 4 in a magic ring {4}

R2: [Inc] 4 times. {8}

R3: [Inc, ssc] 4 times. {12}

R4: [ssc 2, Inc] 4 times. {16}

R5: ssc, [Inc, ssc 3] 3 times, Inc, ssc 2. {20}

R6: ssc 3, [Inc, ssc 4] 3 times, Inc, ssc. {24}

R7: [ssc 5, Inc] 4 times. {28}

R8: [Inc, ssc6] 4 times. {32}

R9: ssc 2, [Inc, ssc 7] 3 times, Inc, ssc 5. {36}

R10: ssc 4, [Inc, ssc 8] 3 times, Inc, ssc 4. {40}

R11: ssc 6, [Inc, ssc 9] 3 times, Inc, ssc 3. {44}

R12: ssc 8, [Inc, ssc 10] 3 times, Inc, ssc 2 {48}

R13: ssc around. {48}

Colorwork begins here (GR – Gray, WH – White, BL – Black)

R14: GR [ssc 20], WH [ssc 3], GR [ssc 2], WH [ssc 3], GR [ssc 20]. {48}

R15: GR [ssc 18], WH [ssc 5], GR [ssc 2], WH [ssc 5], GR [ssc 18]. {48}

R16: GR [ssc 17], WH [ssc 6], GR [ssc 2], WH [ssc 6], GR [ssc 17]. {48}

R17: GR [ssc 16], WH [ssc 7], GR [ssc 2], WH [ssc 7], GR [ssc 16]. {48}

R18: GR [ssc 15], WH [ssc 5], BL [ssc 2], WH [ssc 1], GR [ssc 2], WH [ssc 1], BL [ssc 2], WH [ssc 5], GR [ssc 15]. {48}

R19: GR [ssc 15], WH [ssc 3], BL [ssc 4], WH [ssc 1], GR [ssc 2], WH [ssc 1], BL [ssc 4], WH [ssc 3], GR [ssc 15]. {48}

R20: GR [ssc 14], WH [ssc 3], BL [ssc 5], WH [ssc 1], GR [ssc 2], WH [ssc 1], BL [ssc 5], WH [ssc 3], GR [ssc 14]. {48}

R21 – R25: GR [ssc 14], WH [ssc 2], BL [ssc 16], WH [ssc 2], GR [ssc 14]. {48}

R26: GR [ssc 15], WH [ssc 2], BL [ssc 14], WH [ssc 2], GR [ssc 15]. {48}

R27: GR [ssc 16], WH [ssc], BL [ssc 14], WH [ssc], GR [ssc 16]. {48}

R28: GR [ssc 18], BL [ssc 12], GR [ssc 18].{48}

Change to Gray yarn only:

R29: [Dec, ssc 10] 4 times {44}

R30: ssc 4, [Dec, ssc 9] 3 times, Dec, ssc 5. {40}

R31: [ssc 8, Dec] 4 times. {36}

R32: ssc 2, [Dec, ssc 4] 5 times, Dec, ssc 2. {30}

R33: [Dec, ssc 3] 6 times. {24}

R34: [ssc 2, Dec] 6 times. {18}

Install safety eyes with white circle felt pieces

Neaten the stranded yarns if needed (refer Pic 1 and 2)

Stuff

R35: [ssc, Dec] 6 times. {12}

R36: [Dec] 6 times. {6}

Fasten off and leave a long tail for sewing.

Muzzle

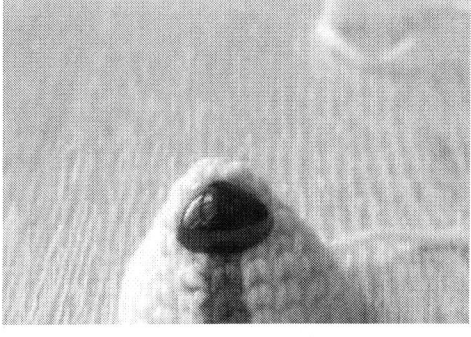

Animals Amigurumi

With White yarn

R1: sc 4 in a magic ring {4}

R2: Inc, ssc 2, Inc. {6}

R3: Inc 2 times, ssc, 1 ch, ssc, Inc. {9}

Colorwork begins here (GR – Gray, WH – White)

R4: WH [ssc 3, Inc, ssc], GR [ssc], WH [ssc, Inc 2 times]. {12}

R5: WH [ssc 3, Inc, ssc 2], GR [ssc], WH [ssc 2, Inc, ssc, Inc]. {15}

R6: WH [Inc, ssc 3, Inc, ssc 2], GR [ssc], WH [ssc 3, Inc, ssc 3]. {18}

R7: WH [Inc, ssc 4, Inc, ssc 3], GR [ssc], WH [ssc 3, Inc, ssc 4]. {21}

R8 – R9: WH [ssc 11], GR [ssc], WH [ssc 9]. {21}

Fasten off and leave a long tail for sewing.

Install safety nose through the ch st at R3.

Ear, make 2

With White yarn:

R1: sc 3 in a magic ring {3}

R2: [Inc] 3 times. {6}

Colorwork begins here (GR – Gray, BL – Black, WH – White)

R3: WH [Inc, ssc], BL [Inc], WH [ssc, Inc, ssc]. {9}

R4: WH [ssc, Inc, ssc], BL [ssc, Inc], WH [ssc 2, Inc, ssc]. {12}

R5: GR [ssc, Inc, ssc 2], BL [ssc, Inc, ssc], GR [ssc 2, Inc, ssc 2]. {15}

R6 – R10: GR [ssc 5], BL [ssc 4], GR [ssc 6]. {15}

Fasten off and leave a long tail for sewing.

Body

With Gray yarn:

R1: sc 6 in a magic ring {6}

R2: [Inc] 6 times. {12}

R3: [ssc 2, Inc] 4 times. {16}

R4: ssc, [Inc, ssc 3] 3 times, Inc, ssc 2. {20}

R5: ssc 3, [Inc, ssc 4] 3 times, Inc, ssc. {24}

R6: [ssc 5, Inc] 4 times. {28}

R7: [Inc, ssc6] 4 times. {32}

R8: ssc 2, [Inc, ssc 7] 3 times, Inc, ssc 5. {36}

R9: ssc 4, [Inc, ssc 8] 3 times, Inc, ssc 4. {40}

R10: ssc 6, [Inc, ssc 9] 3 times, Inc, ssc 3. {44}

Colorwork begins here (GR – Gray, WH – White)

R11: GR [ssc 20], WH [ssc 4], GR [ssc 20]. {44}

R12: GR [ssc 18], WH [ssc 8], GR [ssc 18]. {44}

R13 – R14: GR [ssc 17], WH [ssc 10], GR [ssc 17]. {44}

R15 – R16: GR [ssc 16], WH [ssc 12], GR [ssc 16]. {44}

R17: GR [ssc 10, Dec, ssc 4], WH [ssc 12], GR [ssc 4, Dec, ssc 10]. {42}

R18: GR [ssc 12, Dec, ssc], WH [ssc 12], GR [ssc, Dec, ssc 12]. {40}

R19: GR [ssc 7, Dec, ssc 5], WH [ssc 12], GR [ssc 5, Dec, ssc 7]. {38}

R20: GR [ssc 3, Dec, ssc 8], WH [ssc 12], GR [ssc 8, Dec, ssc 3]. {36}

R21: GR [ssc 9, Dec, ssc 2], WH [ssc 10], GR [ssc 2, Dec, ssc 9]. {34}

R22: GR [ssc 5, Dec, ssc 5], WH [ssc 10], GR [ssc 5, Dec, ssc 5]. {32}

R23: GR [ssc, Dec, ssc 9], WH [ssc 8], GR [ssc 9, Dec, ssc]. {30}

R24: GR [ssc 9, Dec, ssc 2], WH [ssc 4], GR [ssc 2, Dec, ssc 9]. {28}

Change to Gray yarn only:

R25: ssc 5, Dec, ssc 14, Dec, ssc 5. {26}

R26: [ssc 11, Dec] 2 times. {24}

R27: ssc, Dec, ssc 18, Dec, ssc. {22}

R28: ssc 6, [Dec, ssc 6] 2 times. {20}

R29: ssc 2, Dec, ssc 12, Dec, ssc 2.{18}

Neaten stranded yarns if needed

Stuff

R30: [ssc 7, Dec] 2 times. {16}

R31: ssc 3, Dec, ssc 6, Dec, ssc 3. {14}

R32: [ssc 5, Dec] 2 times. {12}

R33: [Dec] 6 times. {6}

Fasten off and leave a long tail for sewing.

Arm and Finger, make 2

Right-hand Fingers

With Black yarn:

[ch 4, slst in 2nd ch from hook, slst in next 2 sts] 4 times to make 4 fingers, [ch 3, slst in 2nd ch from hook, slst in next st] to make a thumb.

ch 1, draw 5 loops, yo and draw through the loops, slst.
Fasten off and leave a long tail for sewing.

Left-hand Fingers

With Black yarn:

[ch 3, slst in 2nd ch from hook, slst in next st] to make a thumb, [ch 4, slst in 2nd ch from hook, slst in next 2 sts] 4 times to make 4 fingers.

ch 1, draw 5 loops, yo and draw through the loops, slst.

Fasten off and leave a long tail for sewing.

Arm

With Gray yarn:

R1: sc 4 in a magic ring {4}

R2: [Inc] 4 times. {8}

R3 – R20: ssc around. {8}

Fasten off and leave a long tail for sewing.

Stuff

Sew the Finger to the Arm.

Leg, make 2

With Black yarn:

R1: sc 6 in a magic ring {6}

R2: [Inc] 6 times. {12}

R3: [ssc 2, Inc] 4 times. {16}

R4: ssc, [Inc, ssc 3] 3 times, Inc, ssc 2. {20}

R5 – R7: ssc around. {20}

R8: ssc, [Dec, ssc 3] 3 times, Dec, ssc 2. {16}

R9: [ssc 2, Dec] 4 times. {12}

R10 – R13: ssc around. {12}

Change to Gray yarn only:

R14 – R17: ssc around. {12}

Fasten off and leave a long tail for sewing.

Stuff

Tail

With Black yarn:

R1: sc 3 in a magic ring {3}

R2: [Inc] 3 times. {6}

R3: ssc around. {6}

Change to Gray yarn:

R4: [Inc, ssc] 3 times. {9}

R5: [ssc 2, Inc] 3 times. {12}

R6: ssc, [Inc, ssc 3] 2 times, Inc, ssc 2. {15}

Change to Black yarn:

R7: ssc 3, [Inc, ssc 4] 2 times, Inc, ssc. {18}

R8: [ssc 5, Inc] 3 times. {21}

R9: [Inc, ssc6] 3 times. {24}

Change to Gray yarn:

R10 – R12: ssc around. {24}

Change to Black yarn:

R13 – R15: ssc around. {24}

Change to Gray yarn:

R16 – R18: ssc around. {24}

Change to Black yarn:

R19: [Dec, ssc 6] 3 times. {21}

R20: ssc around. {21}

R21: ssc 2, [Dec, ssc 5] 2 times, Dec, ssc 3. {18}

Animals Amigurumi

Change to Gray yarn:

R22: ssc around. {18}

R23: [ssc 4, Dec] 3 times. {15}

R24: ssc around. {15}

Change to Black yarn:

Stuff

R25: [Dec, ssc 3] 3 times. {12}

R26: ssc around. {12}

R27: [ssc 2, Dec] 3 times. {9}

Change to Gray yarn:

R28: ssc around. {9}

R29: [Dec, ssc], 3 times. {6}

R30: ssc around. {6}

Fasten off and leave a long tail for sewing.

Raccoon Amigurumi: Assembly

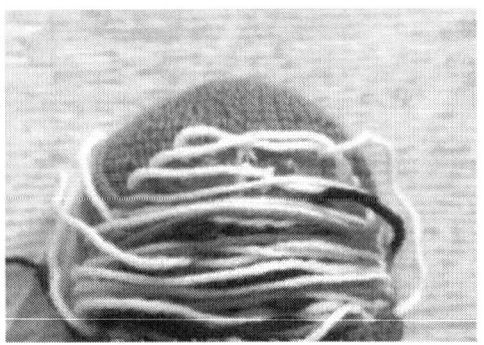

Pic 1

This is how the inside of the colorwork amigurumi looks. You may leave the unworked yarn stranded as it is. If you have left a decent length of yarn between the colorwork, then you are fine to leave them as it is. If the yarns are too short, you may trim the yarn and knot them together as shown in Pic 2.

Pic 2

Personally, I prefer to neaten my lengthy unworked yarn stranded across the colorwork section. The clean interior makes it easier for stuffing and shaping.

Align the muzzle of the raccoon amigurumi with the marking between the eyes as shown in the picture. Pin, sew while stuffing the muzzle to the head.

Next, position and pin the ears to the head. Make sure bother ears are aligned and in symmetry.

Position all parts together. First, sew the head to the body, followed by the arms, legs, and tail respectively.

Jr. Rakku, the Raccoon Amigurumi loves the fall season. He is waiting for the leaves to fall so that he could go out to collect as much maple leaves as he can.

I just love how Jr. Rakku's tail turns out to be, strippy black and gray

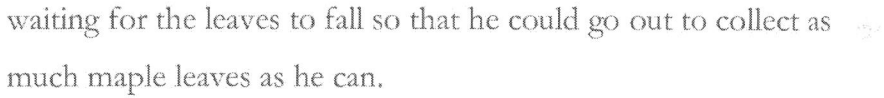

Animals Amigurumi

DEER AMIGURUMI PATTERN

Height: 10" tall

Skill level: Intermediate

Duration: About 8 hours

Description:

DuDu, the Deer Amigurumi, a cute young deer who has just moved into the woodland. Due to nature and her species, predators hunt them for meat, human hunt them for game and meat. She does not want to be hunted down so she decided to leave her family and move into the woodland seeking for Mr. Furu's assistance, with the intention to learn as many new survival skills as she possibly can. We wish her all the best!

Abbreviations

Crochet (in US Terms)

ch: chain

sc: single crochet

ssc = split single crochet / knit stitch / waistcoat stitch

Inc: 2ssc increase

Dec: ssc 2 stitches together

slst: slip stitch

Others

R: Round

BR: Brown Yarn

BE: Beige Yarn

BL: Black Yarn

WH: White Yarn

Animals Amigurumi

Materials

1. 3.5mm hook
2. Acrylic yarn (50 gram each ball): White, Black, Beige (or Light Khaki) and Brown (1 ball)
3. Colored Iris Safety Eyes, Gray, 10mm size, 2
4. Safety Nose, 18mm size, 1
5. Darning needle
6. Polyester fiberfill
7. Scissors
8. Pins

Important Note: This is a colorwork amigurumi using Split Single Crochet / Knit Stitch / Waistcoat Stitch method. Please DO NOT attempt to convert it to normal Single Crochet.

Why use Split Sing Crochet instead of normal Single Crochet?
Please take note that this amigurumi pattern is using Split Single Crochet (SSC), some may know it as Crochet Knit Stitch or Waistcoat Stitch. Unlike the normal Single Crochet, SSC inserts hook in between the legs of the next st. In colorwork amigurumi where stitches are crochet in the continuous round, SSC keeps the colorwork vertically straight throughout the round. It is because the

hook is inserted in between the legs of next stitch, but if you are using normal Single Crochet, the colorwork will lean to the right or left depending on if you are right-handed or left-handed.

How to change yarn color in colorwork crochet?
Follow the pattern to work on stitches in color A until the last yarn over, pull through the loop with the new color B. Leave the color A behind until it is time to work on it again. Continue to work in Color B until it is time to change the color back to A, on the last stitch in the color B, just pull through the color A on the last yarn over and drop the color B. Leave a decent length of the unwork yarn between the color change so that it won't distort the shape of your amigurumi. Repeat this until you have completed the pattern.
Note: I don't hide the unworked yarn between the stitches because it will cause distortion in stitch height, especially in SSC stitch.

Deer Amigurumi: Crochet Pattern

Head

With Brown yarn:

R1: sc 4 in a magic ring {4}

R2: [Inc] 4 times. {8}

R3: [Inc, ssc] 4 times. {12}

R4: [ssc 2, Inc] 4 times. {16}

R5: ssc, [Inc, ssc 3] 3 times, Inc, ssc 2. {20}

R6: ssc 3, [Inc, ssc 4] 3 times, Inc, ssc. {24}

R7: [ssc 5, Inc] 4 times. {28}

R8: [Inc, ssc6] 4 times. {32}

R9: ssc 2, [Inc, ssc 7] 3 times, Inc, ssc 5. {36}

R10: ssc 4, [Inc, ssc 8] 3 times, Inc, ssc 4. {40}

R11: ssc 6, [Inc, ssc 9] 3 times, Inc, ssc 3. {44}

R12: ssc 8, [Inc, ssc 10] 3 times, Inc, ssc 2 {48}

R13: sc around. {48}

Colorwork begins here (BR- Brown, BE – Beige, WH – White)

R14: BR [ssc 16], BE [ssc 5], BR [ssc 7], BE [ssc 5], BR [ssc 15]. {48}

R15: BR [ssc 16], BE [ssc 6], BR [ssc 5], BE [ssc 6], BR [ssc 15]. {48}

R16: BR [ssc 15], BE [ssc 7], BR [ssc 5], BE [ssc 7], BR [ssc 14]. {48}

R17: BR [ssc 15], BE [ssc 8], BR [ssc 3], BE [ssc 8], BR [ssc 14]. {48}

R18: BR [ssc 15], BE [ssc 8], BR [ssc 3], BE [ssc 8], BR [ssc 14]. {48}

R19: BR [ssc 15], BE [ssc 3], WH [ssc 3], BE [ssc 3], BR [ssc 1], BE [ssc 3], WH [ssc 3], BE [ssc 3], BR [ssc 14]. {48}

R20: BR [ssc 14], BE [ssc 4], WH [ssc 3], BE [ssc 3], BR [ssc 1], BE [ssc 3], WH [ssc 3], BE [ssc 4], BR [ssc 13]. {48}

R21 – R22: BR [ssc 14], BE [ssc 3], WH [ssc 5], BE [ssc 2], BR [ssc 1], BE [ssc 2], WH [ssc 5], BE [ssc 3], BR [ssc 13]. {48}

R23 – R25: BR [ssc 14], BE [ssc 3], WH [ssc 5], BE [ssc 5], WH [ssc 5], BE [ssc 3], BR [ssc 13]. {48}

R26: BR [ssc 14], BE [ssc 4], WH [ssc 3], BE [ssc 7], WH [ssc 3], BE [ssc 4], BR [ssc 13]. {48}

R27: BR [ssc 16], BE [ssc 17], BR [ssc 15]. {48}

R28: BR [ssc 18], BE [ssc 13], BR [ssc 17]. {48}

Change to Brown yarn only:

R29: [Dec, ssc 10] 4 times {44}

R30: ssc 4, [Dec, ssc 9] 3 times, Dec, ssc 5. {40}

R31: [ssc 8, Dec] 4 times. {36}

R32: ssc 2, [Dec, ssc 4] 5 times, Dec, ssc 2. {30}

R33: [Dec, ssc 3] 6 times. {24}

R34: [ssc 2, Dec] 6 times. {18}

Install safety eyes

Neaten the stranded yarns if needed (refer Pic 1 and 2)

Stuff

R35: [ssc, Dec] 6 times. {12}

R36: [Dec] 6 times. {6}

Fasten off and leave a long tail for sewing.

Muzzle

With Beige yarn

R1: sc 4 in a magic ring {4}

R2: Inc, ssc 2, Inc. {6}

R3: Inc 2 times, ssc, 1 ch, ssc, Inc. {9}

Colorwork begins here (BE – Beige, BR – Brown)

R4: BE [ssc 3, Inc, ssc], BR [ssc], BE [ssc, Inc 2 times]. {12}

R5: BE [ssc 3, Inc, ssc 2], BR [ssc], BE [ssc 2, Inc, ssc, Inc]. {15}

R6: BE [Inc, ssc 3, Inc, ssc 2], BR [ssc], BE [ssc 3, Inc, ssc 3]. {18}

R7: BE [Inc, ssc 4, Inc, ssc 3], BR [ssc], BE [ssc 3, Inc, ssc 4]. {21}

R8 – R9: BE [ssc 11], BR [ssc], BE [ssc 9]. {21}

Fasten off and leave a long tail for sewing.

Install safety nose through the ch st at R3.

Ear, make 2

With Black yarn:

R1: sc 3 in a magic ring {3}

R2: [Inc] 3 times. {6}

Colorwork begins here (BR – Brown, BE – Beige)

R3: BR [Inc, ssc], BE [Inc], BR [ssc, Inc, ssc]. {9}

R4: BR [ssc, Inc, ssc], BE [ssc, Inc], BR [ssc 2, Inc, ssc]. {12}

R5: BR [ssc, Inc, ssc 2], BE [ssc, Inc, ssc], BR [ssc 2, Inc, ssc 2]. {15}

R6: BR [ssc, Inc, ssc 3], BE [ssc, Inc, ssc 2], BR [ssc 2, Inc, ssc 3]. {18}

R7 – R13: BR [ssc 6], BE [ssc 5], BR [ssc 7]. {18}

Fasten off and leave a long tail for sewing.

Fold the ear vertically and sew the base (shown as the left ear in the picture), repeat for both ears

Body

With Brown yarn:

R1: sc 6 in a magic ring {6}

R2: [Inc] 6 times. {12}

R3: [ssc 2, Inc] 4 times. {16}

R4: ssc, [Inc, ssc 3] 3 times, Inc, ssc 2. {20}

R5: ssc 3, [Inc, ssc 4] 3 times, Inc, ssc. {24}

R6: [ssc 5, Inc] 4 times. {28}

R7: [Inc, ssc6] 4 times. {32}

R8: ssc 2, [Inc, ssc 7] 3 times, Inc, ssc 5. {36}

R9: ssc 4, [Inc, ssc 8] 3 times, Inc, ssc 4. {40}

R10: ssc 6, [Inc, ssc 9] 3 times, Inc, ssc 3. {44}

R11: ssc around {44}

Colorwork begins here (BR – Brown, BE – Beige)

R12: BR [ssc 19], BE [ssc 6], BR [ssc 19]. {44}

R13: BR [ssc 18], BE [ssc 8], BR [ssc 18]. {44}

R14 – R16: BR [ssc 17], BE [ssc 10], BR [ssc 17]. {44}

R17: BR [ssc 10, Dec, ssc 5], BE [ssc 10], BR [ssc 5, Dec, ssc 7], BE [ssc], BR [ssc 2]. {42}

R18: BR [ssc 2], BE [ssc], BR [ssc 10, Dec, ssc 2], BE [ssc 8], BR [ssc 2, Dec, ssc 13]. {40}

R19: BR [Dec, ssc 14], BE [ssc 3, Dec, ssc 3], BR [ssc 11], BE [ssc], BR [ssc 3], BE [ssc]. {38}

R20: BR [ssc 3], BE [ssc], BR [ssc 2, Dec, ssc 7], BE [ssc 7], BR [ssc 7, Dec, ssc 7]. {36}

R21: BR [ssc 11, Dec, ssc], BE [ssc 7], BR [ssc, Dec, ssc 9], BE [ssc], BR [ssc 2]. {34}

R22: BR [ssc], BE [ssc], BR [ssc 11], BE [ssc 2, Dec, ssc 3], BR [ssc

12, Dec]. {32}

R23: BR [ssc 3, Dec, ssc 8], BE [ssc 6], BR [ssc 6, Dec, ssc], BE [ssc], BR [ssc 3]. {30}

R24: BR [ssc 3], BE [ssc], BR [ssc 3, Dec, ssc 4], BE [ssc 4], BR [ssc 4, Dec, ssc 7]. {28}

R25: BR [ssc 4, Dec, ssc 6], BE [ssc 4], BR [ssc 6, Dec, ssc 2], BE [ssc], BR [ssc]. {26}

R26: BR [ssc], BE [ssc], BR [ssc 6, Dec, ssc], BE [ssc 4], BR [ssc, Dec, ssc 8]. {24}

R27: BR [Dec, ssc 8], BE [ssc, Dec, ssc], BR [ssc 6], BE [ssc], BR [ssc 2], BE [ssc]. {22}

R28: BR [ssc 2], BE [ssc], BR [Dec, ssc 4], BE [ssc 3], BR [ssc 4, Dec, ssc 4]. {20}

R29: BR [ssc 6, Dec], BE [ssc 3], BR [Dec, ssc 5], BE [ssc], BR [ssc]. {18}

Neaten stranded yarns if needed

Stuff

R30: BE [ssc], BR [ssc 3, Dec, ssc], BE [ssc 3], BR [ssc, Dec, ssc 5]. {16}

R31: BR [ssc, Dec, ssc 3], BE [ssc 3], BR [ssc 3, Dec, ssc 2]. {14}

R32: BR [ssc 2, Dec, ssc], BE [ssc 3], BR [ssc 2, Dec, ssc 2]. {12}

Change to Brown yarn only:

R33: [Dec] 6 times. {6}

Fasten off and leave a long tail for sewing.

Arm, make 2

With Black yarn:

R1: sc 4 in a magic ring {4}

R2: [Inc] 4 times. {8}

R3: [Inc, ssc] 4 times. {12}

R4: [ssc 2, Inc] 4 times. {16}

R5 – R6 : ssc around {16}

R7: [Dec, ssc 2] 4 times. {12}

R8: [ssc, Dec] 4 times. {8}

Change to Beige yarn only:

R9: ssc around. {8}

Change to Brown yarn only:

R10 – R24: ssc around. {8}

Fasten off and leave a long tail for sewing.

Stuff

Leg, make 2

Animals Amigurumi

With Black yarn:

R1: sc 6 in a magic ring {6}

R2: [Inc] 6 times. {12}

R3: [ssc 2, Inc] 4 times. {16}

R4: ssc, [Inc, ssc 3] 3 times, Inc, ssc 2. {20}

R5 – R7: ssc around. {20}

R8: ssc, [Dec, ssc 3] 3 times, Dec, ssc 2. {16}

R9: [ssc 2, Dec] 4 times. {12}

Change to Beige yarn only:

R10: ssc around. {12}

Leave a long tail for sewing

Change to Brown yarn only:

R11 – R17: ssc around. {12}

Fasten off and leave a long tail for sewing.

Stuff

Sew a vertical line with Beige yarn at the foot (As shown in the picture)

Tail

With Brown yarn:

R1: sc 3 in a magic ring {3}

R2: [Inc] 3 times. {6}

Colorwork begins here (BR – Brown, BE – Beige)

R3: BR [Inc, ssc], BE [Inc], BR [ssc, Inc, ssc]. {9}

R4: BR [ssc, Inc, ssc], BE [ssc, Inc], BR [ssc 2, Inc, ssc]. {12}

R5 – R9: BR [ssc 4], BE [ssc 3], BR [ssc 5]. {12}

Fasten off and leave a long tail for sewing.

Deer Amigurumi: Assembly

Pic 1

This is how the inside of the colorwork amigurumi looks. You may leave the unworked yarn stranded as it is. If you have left a decent length of yarn between the colorwork, then you are fine to leave them as it is. If the yarns are too short, you may trim the yarn and knot them together as shown in Pic 2.

Pic 2

Personally, I prefer to neaten my lengthy unworked yarn instead of stranded across the colorwork section. The clean interior makes it easier for stuffing and shaping.

Align the muzzle of the deer amigurumi with the marking between the eyes as shown in the picture. Pin, sew and stuff the muzzle to the head.

Next, position and pin the ears to the head. Make sure bother ears are aligned and in symmetry.

Position all parts together. First, sew the head to the body, followed by the arms, legs, and tail respectively.

Animals Amigurumi

DuDu Deer Amigurumi is ready to explore her new environment in the woodland. She needs more loves and courage from you. Please share this pattern with your friends who love to make crochet toys.

Hope you like her and happy crochet! ~XOXO

ELEPHANT AMIGURUMI CROCHET PATTERN

Materials

Elephant

- 2.5mm hook
- Acrylic yarn in Grey (for Elwis) or Cyan (for Elyra), Pink, Pastel Pink & White colors

Animals Amigurumi

- Polyester fiberfill
- 10mm Dome-Button Eye, 1 pair

Diaper Pants

- 2.5mm hook
- Acrylic yarn in Blue and White colors
- Small buttons (7/16" - 1/2"), 2 pcs.

Dress

- 2.5mm hook
- Acrylic yarn in rainbow color

Tools

- Darning needle (Long)
- Fabric marker (water erasable), optional for position marking
- Scissors
- Pins

Instructions

1. Crochet all parts by following the crochet patterns stated below.
2. Stuff and sew the parts as instructed.

3. For head, sew dome-button eyes. If you are making Elwis with the trunk-up position, sew the mouth and tusks on the head too.
4. Sew the ears and body to the head followed by sewing arms, feet, and tail to the body to complete the elephant amigurumi.

~ . ~ . ~ . ~ . ~

Abbreviations

BLO: back loop only

ch: chain

dc: double crochet

FLO: front loop only

hdc: half double crochet

inc: 2sc increase

inv dec: invisible decrease

sc: single crochet

sc2tog: sc2 together (normal decreasing stitch)

slst: slip stitch

st: stitch

~.~.~.~.~

AMIGURUMI PATTERN

Elwis is crochet from Grey Yarn and Elyra is crochet from Cyan Yarn. Both Elephants are crochet from the same pattern, while Elwis's trunk is pointing upward and Elyra's trunk is pointing downward. However, the major differences between them are 1. Elyra doesn't have tusks and mouth, also, 2. Elyra is wearing a dress and Elwis is wearing removable diaper pants. The dress is done by adding ruffle pieces to the bottom and top of the body, at the same time, part of the body is crochet from the same yarn as the ruffle pieces.

BODY

the base of the

body.

(This pattern is for the bare body. Refer Dress pattern for Elyra that wears a dress)

With Grey yarn:

Round 1: ch5, Inc in 2nd ch from hook, sc 2, 5sc in the last ch. Continue on the other side of the chain base, sc 2, 3sc in the last ch. {14}

Round 2: Inc, sc 4, [Inc] 3 times, sc 4, [Inc] 2 times. {20}

Round 3: Inc, sc 6, [Inc] 2 times, sc, Inc, sc 6, [Inc] 2 times, sc. {26}

Round 4: Inc, sc 8, [Inc, sc] 2 times, Inc, sc 8, [Inc, sc] 2 times. {32}

Round 5: Inc, sc 10, Inc, sc 2, Inc, sc, Inc, sc 10, Inc, sc 2, Inc, sc. {38}

Round 6: Inc. sc 12, [Inc, sc 2] 2 times, Inc, sc 12, [Inc, sc 2] 2 times. {44}

Round 7: Inc, sc 14, Inc, sc 3, Inc, sc 2, Inc, sc 14, Inc, sc 3, Inc, sc 2. {50}

Round 8: Inc, sc 16, [Inc, sc 3] 2 times, Inc, sc 16, [Inc, sc 3] 2 times. {56}

Round 9: sc around. {56}

Round 10: sc 25, Inc, sc 27, Inc, sc 2. {58}

Round 11: sc 26, Inc, sc 28, Inc, sc 2. {60}

Round 12: sc 27, Inc, sc 29, Inc, sc 2. {62}

Round 13: sc 28, Inc, sc 30, Inc, sc 2. {64}

Round 14 – 23: sc around. {64}

Round 24: sc 6, [Inv dec, sc 14] 3 times, Inv dec, sc 8. {60}

Round 25: sc around. {60}

Round 26: sc 6, [Inv dec, sc 13] 3 times, Inv dec, sc 7. {56}

Round 27: sc around. {56}

Round 28: sc 6, [Inv dec, sc 12] 3 times, Inv dec, sc 6. {52}

Round 29: sc around. {52}

Round 30: sc 6, [Inv dec, sc 11] 3 times, Inv dec, sc 5. {48}

Round 31: sc around. {48}

Round 32: sc 6, [Inv dec, sc 10] 3 times, Inv dec, sc 4. {44}

Round 33: sc around. {44}

Round 34: sc 6, [Inv dec, sc 9] 3 times, Inv dec, sc 3. {40}

Round 35: sc around. {40}

Round 36: sc 6, [Inv dec, sc 8] 3 times, Inv dec, sc 2. {36}

Round 37: sc around. {36}

Round 38: [sc 4, Inv dec] around. {30}

Stuff the body firmly with polyester fiberfill.

Round 39: sc around. {30}

Round 40: sc 2, [Inv dec, sc 3] 5 times, inv dec, sc. {24}

Round 41: [sc 2, Inv dec] around. {18}

Round 42: [Inv dec, sc] around. {12}

Round 43: [Inv dec] around. {6}

Fasten and leave a long tail for sewing.

#

HEAD

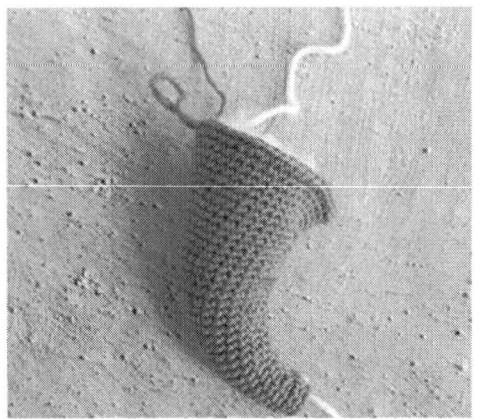

The trunk, at Round 36.

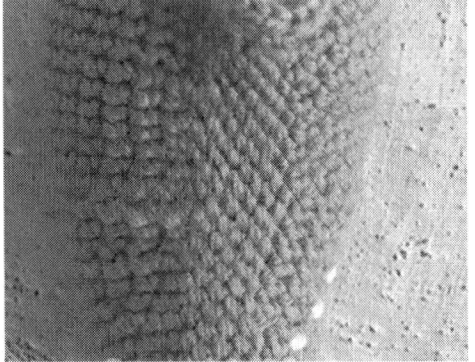

slst FLO stitches

on the trunk that makes it curls.

Animals Amigurumi

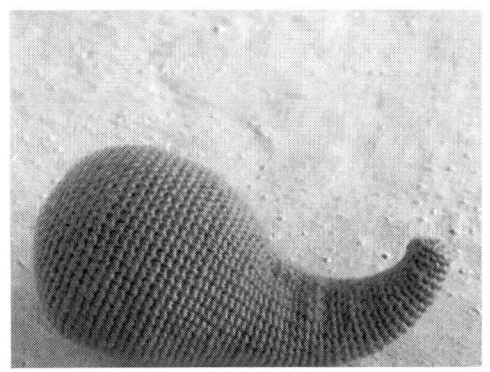

With Grey yarn:

Round 1: Sc 6 in magic ring. {6}

Round 2: [inc] around. {12}

Round 3: sc around BLO. {12}

Round 4: sc 10, slst FLO 2. {12}

Round 5: slst FLO 2, sc 8, slst FLO 2. {12}

Round 6: slst FLO 2, [inc, sc 2] 3 times, slst FLO 1. {15}

Round 7 - 9: slst FLO 3, sc 11, slst FLO 1. {15}

Round 10: slst FLO 4, [inc, sc 3] 2 times, inc, sc 2. {18}

Round 11 - 13: slst FLO 4, sc 14. {18}

Round 14: sc, slst FLO 4, [inc, sc 4] 2 times, inc, sc 2. {21}

Round 15 - 16: sc, slst FLO 4, sc 16. {21}

Stuff with polyester fillings.

Round 17: inc, sc, slst FLO 4, sc, [inc, sc 6] 2 times. {24}

Round 18 - 19: sc 3, slst FLO 4, sc 17. {24}

Round 20: inc, sc 2, slst FLO 5, [inc, sc 7] 2 times. {27}

Round 21 - 22: sc 4, slst FLO 5, sc 18. {27}

Round 23: inc, sc 3, slst FLO 5, [inc, sc 8] 2 times. {30}

Round 24 - 25: sc 6, slst FLO 5, sc 19. {30}

Round 26: sc 2, inc, sc 4, slst FLO 5, inc, sc 9, inc, sc 7. {33}

Round 27: sc 8, slst FLO 5, sc 20. {33}

Round 28: sc 2, inc, sc 5, slst FLO 5, inc, sc 10, inc, sc 8. {36}

Round 29: sc 10, slst FLO 5, sc 21. {36}

Round 30: sc 3, inc, sc 6, slst FLO 5, inc, sc 11, inc, sc 8. {39}

Round 31: sc 12, slst FLO 5, sc 22. {39}

Round 32: sc 4, inc, sc 7, slst FLO 5, inc, sc 12, inc, sc 8. {42}

Round 33 - 35: sc 13, slst FLO 5, sc 24. {42}

Round 36: [inc, sc 6] around. {48}

Stuff with polyester fillings.

Round 37: sc around. {48}

Round 38: [inc, sc 7] around. {54}

Round 39 - 40: sc around. {54}

Round 41: sc 4, [inc, sc 8] 5 times, inc, sc 4. {60}

Round 42 - 43: sc around. {60}

Round 44: [inc, sc 9] around. {66}

Round 45 - 51: sc around. {66}

Round 52: [inv dec, sc 9] around. {60}

Round 53: sc around. {60}

Round 54: sc 4, [inv dec, sc 8] 5 times, inv dec, sc 4. {54}

Round 55: sc around. {54}

Round 56: [inv dec, sc 7] around. {48}

Round 57: sc around. {48}

Round 58: sc 3, [inv dec, sc 6] 5 times, inv dec, sc 3. {42}

Round 59: sc around. {42}

Round 60: [inv dec, sc 5] around. {36}

Round 61: sc around. {36}

Round 62: sc 2, [inv dec, sc 4] 5 times, inv dec, sc 2. {30}

Stuff with polyester fillings.

Round 63: [inv dec, sc 3] around. {24}

Round 64: sc, [inv dec, sc 2] 5 times, inv dec, sc. {18}

Round 65: [inv dec, sc 1] around. {12}

Round 66: [inv dec] around. {6}

Fasten and hide yarn end.

#

MOUTH

Animals Amigurumi

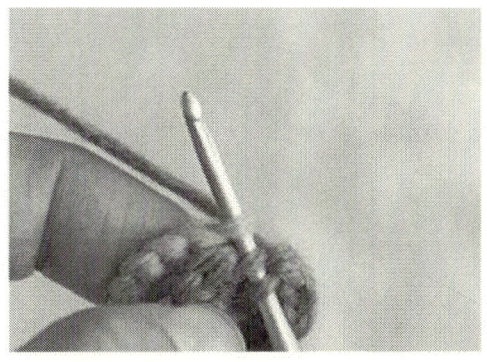

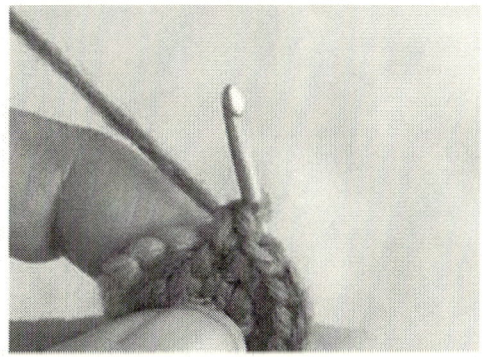

Made from 2 layers of circle pieces.

With Pink Yarn

Round 1: sc 6 in magic ring. {6}

Round 2: [inc] around. {12}

Fasten

With Grey Yarn

Round 1: Sc 6 in magic ring. {6}

Round 2: [inc] around. {12}

Don't fasten and don't cut yarn.

Stake both pink and grey pieces together with the wrong-side on each other, continue to crochet the next round with grey yarn.

Round 3: [inc, sc] around on FLO on both circle pieces. {18}

Fasten.

Fold the mouth and sew a few stitches to give it a scooped appearance.

Leave a long tail for sewing.

#

TUSKS

Animals Amigurumi

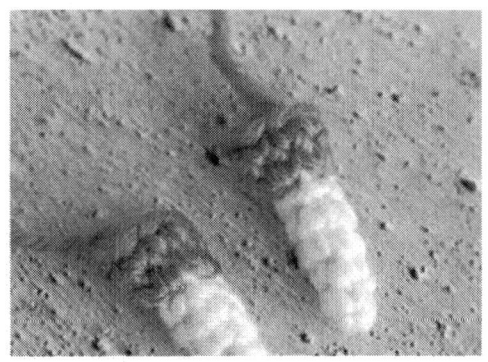

Make 2 with White yarn:

Round 1: Sc 3 in magic ring. {3}

Round 2: sc around. {3}

Round 3: sc, inc, sc {4}

Round 4 - 6: sc around. {4}

Change yarn to Grey color

Round 7: [inc] around. {8}

Round 8: sc around. {8}

Fasten. Leave a long tail for sewing.

#

EARS

Animals Amigurumi

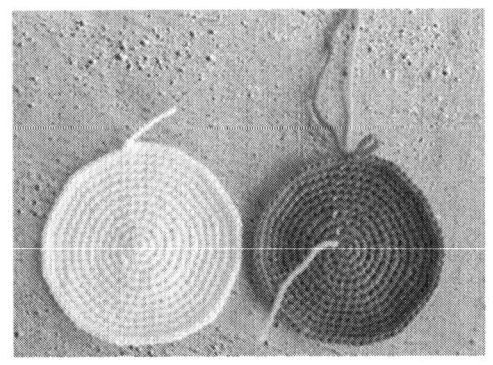

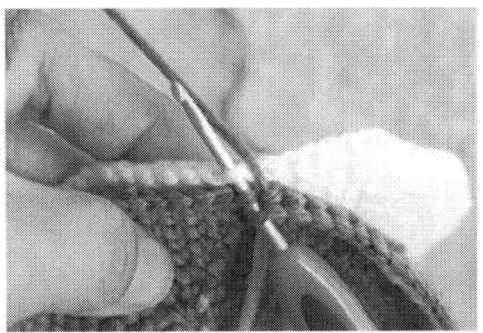

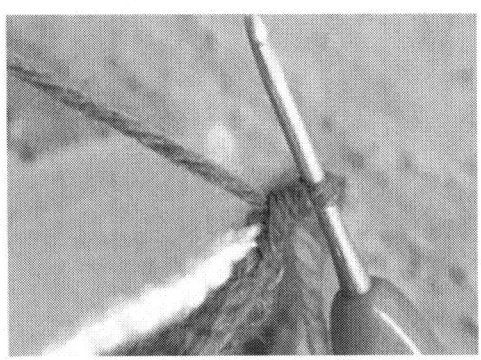

Animals Amigurumi

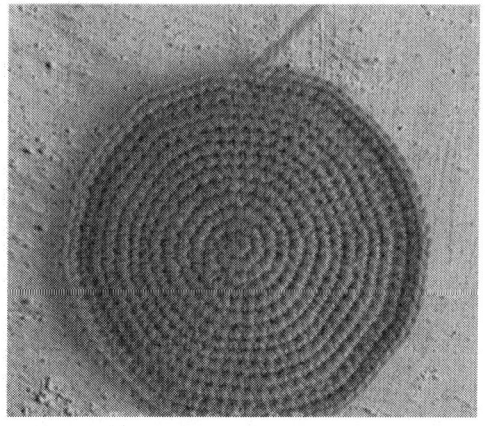

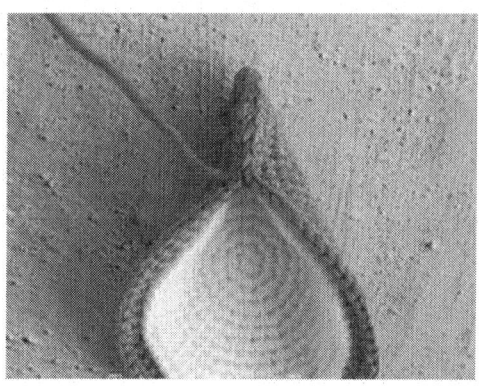

Animals Amigurumi

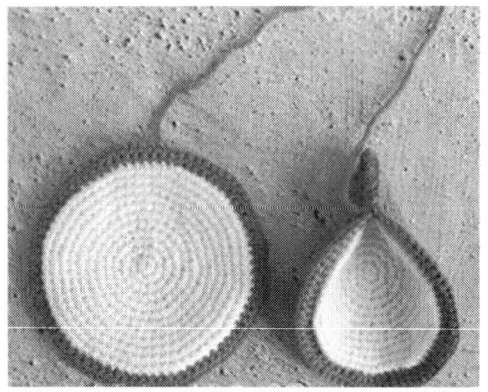

Each ear is made from 2 layers of circle pieces.

Make 2 with Pastel Pink yarn:

Round 1: Sc 6 in magic ring. {6}

Round 2: [inc] around. {12}

Round 3: [inc, sc] around. {18}

Round 4: [sc 2, inc] around. {24}

Round 5: [inc, sc 3] around. {30}

Round 6: sc 2, [inc, sc 4] 5 times, inc, sc 2. {36}

Round 7: [inc, sc 5] around. {42}

Round 8: sc 3, [inc, sc 6] 5 times, inc, sc 3. {48}

Round 9: [inc, sc 7] around. {54}

Round 10: sc 4, [inc, sc 8] 5 times, inc, sc 4. {60}

Round 11: [inc, sc 9] around. {66}

Round 12: sc 5, [inc, sc 10] 5 times, inc, sc 5. { 72}

Fasten.

With Grey yarn:

Round 1 - 12: Follow the ear pattern above.

Don't fasten and don't cut yarn.

Stake both pink and grey pieces together with the wrong-side on each other, continue to crochet the next round with grey yarn.

Round 13: [inc, sc 11] around on FLO on both circle pieces. {80}

Round 14: sc 6, [inc, sc 12] 5 times, inc, sc 6. { 86}

Fasten and leave a long tail for sewing.

Fold the ear and sew both layers together for about 9 to 10 stitches to give it a scooped appearance.

#

ARMS

Make 2 starting with White yarn:

Round 1: sc 6 in magic ring. {6}

Round 2: [inc] around. {12}

Round 3: [inc, sc] around. {18}

Round 4: [sc 2. inc] around. {24}

Round 5: [inc, sc 3] around. {30}

Round 6: sc around. {30}

Change yarn color to Grey:

Round 7: sc BLO around {30}

Round 8 – 10: sc around. {30}

Round 11: [sc 8, Inv dec] around. {27}

Round 12 - 13: sc around. {27}

Sew 4 vertical short lines with 4 strands of white yarn as fingers.

Round 14: [sc 7, Inv dec] around. {24}

Round 15 – 16: sc around. {24}

Round 17: [sc 6, Inv dec] around. {21}

Round 18 – 19: sc around. {21}

Round 20: [sc 5, Inv dec] around. {18}

Round 21 – 22: sc around {18}.

Round 23: [sc 4, Inv dec] around. {15}

Round 24 – 35: sc around. {15}

Note: for Elyra, the elephant that wears a dress, finish the arm 2 rounds shorter, ie. fasten after complete round33.

Fasten and leave a long tail for sewing.

Fill the bottom 2/3 of the arms firmly with polyester fiberfill.

#

LEGS

Make 2 starting with White yarn:

Round 1: ch5, Inc in 2nd ch from hook, sc 2, 5sc in the last ch. Continue on the other side of the chain base, sc 2, 3sc in the last ch. {14}

Round 2: Inc, sc 4, [Inc] 3 times, sc 4, [Inc] 2 times. {20}

Round 3: Inc, sc 6, [Inc] 2 times, sc, Inc, sc 6, [Inc] 2 times, sc. {26}

Round 4: Inc, sc 8, [Inc, sc] 2 times, Inc, sc 8, [Inc, sc] 2 times. {32}

Round 5: Inc, sc 10, Inc, sc 2, Inc, sc, Inc, sc 10, Inc, sc 2, Inc, sc. {38}

Animals Amigurumi

Round 6: Inc. sc 12, [Inc, sc 2] 2 times, Inc, sc 12, [Inc, sc 2] 2 times. {44}

Round 7: sc around {44}

Change yarn color to Grey

Round 8: sc BLO around. {44}

Round 9 – 10: sc around. {44}

Round 11: sc 14, Inv dec, sc 12, Inv dec, sc 14. {42}

Round 12: sc 14, Inv dec, sc 10, Inv dec, sc 14. {40}

Round 13: sc 14, Inv dec, sc 8, Inv dec, sc 14. {38}

Round 14: sc 14, Inv dec, sc 6, Inv dec, sc 14. {36}

Round 15: sc 14, Inv dec, sc 4, Inv dec, sc 14. {34}

Round 16: sc 14, Inv dec, sc 2, Inv dec, sc 14. {32}

Round 17: sc 14, Inv dec, Inv dec, sc 14. {30}

Sew 4 vertical short lines with 4 strands of yarn as toes.

Round 18: sc around. {30}

Round 19: [sc 6, Inv dec] 3 times, sc 6. {27}

Round 20 – 21: sc around. {27}

Round 22: sc 6, [Inv dec, sc 5] 3 times. {24}

Round 23 – 24: sc around. {24}

Round 25: sc 5, Inv dec, sc 10, Inv dec, sc 5. {22}

Round 26 – 27: sc around. {22}

Round 28: sc 5, Inv dec, sc 9, Inv dec, sc 4. {20}

Round 29 – 30: sc around. {20}

Round 31: sc 4, Inv dec, sc 8, Inv dec, sc 4. {18}

Fasten and leave a long tail for sewing.

Fill the bottom 2/3 of the legs firmly with polyester fiberfill.

#

TAIL

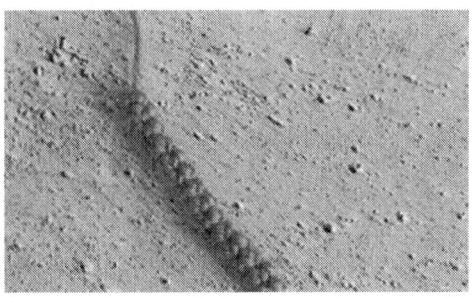

With Grey yarn:

ch 4, slst to form a ring.

ch1, sc 4 into the ring. sc around until the tail is 4" long, slst.

ch3, ps3 in each st, slst.

ch, Inv dec around, slst, ch

Fasten off. Trim near the knot. Apply tiny craft glue to the end and shape it pointy.

#

DIAPER PANTS

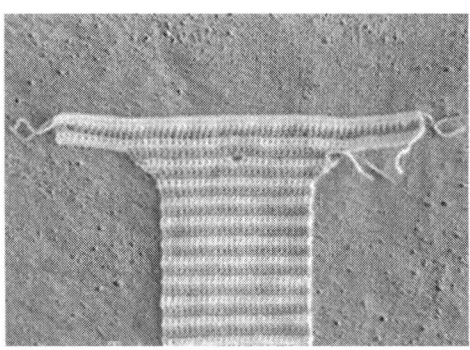

Diaper pants before adding the edging, it has 2 buttonholes and a hole for the tail.

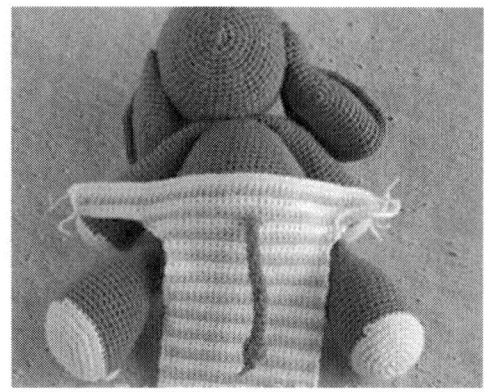

Here is the hole for the tail. The tail was sewed at round 16 on the body, if you sewn it at a different height, the position of the hole might not match with the tail.

With White yarn:

Row 1: ch 61, sc in 2nd st from hook, sc 59 (till you reach the end of the chain stitch), turn. {60}

Row 2: ch, sc 60, turn. {60}

Fasten off.

Change yarn to Blue:

Row 3: ch2 (as 1 hdc), hdc in next st, ch, skip 1 st, hdc in next 54 sts, ch, skip 1 st, hdc in next 2 sts, turn. {60} [button holes are made on this row]

Fasten off.

Change yarn to White:

Row 4 - 5: ch, sc in next 60 sts, turn. {60}

Fasten off.

Change yarn to blue:

Row 6: insert hook in 13th st, ch, sc in the same st, sc in next 36 sts, turn. {36}

Row 7: ch, sc2tog, sc in next 32 sts, sc2tog, turn. {34}

Change yarn to White:

Row 8: ch, sc2tog, sc in next 14 sts, ch 2, skip 2 sts, sc in next 14 sts, sc2tog, turn. {32} [a hole for the elephant tail is made on this row]

Row 9: ch, sc2tog, sc in next 28 sts, sc2tog, turn. {30}

Change yarn to blue:

Row 10: ch, sc2tog, sc in next 26 sts, sc2tog, turn. {28}

Row 11: ch, sc2tog, sc in next 24 sts, sc2tog, turn. {26}

Change yarn to White:

Row 12 - 13: ch, sc in next 26 sts, turn. {26}

Change yarn to blue:

Row 14 - 15: ch, sc in next 26 sts, turn. {26}

Row 16 - 53: Repeat Row 12 - 15.

Fasten off. Hide yarn

Edging

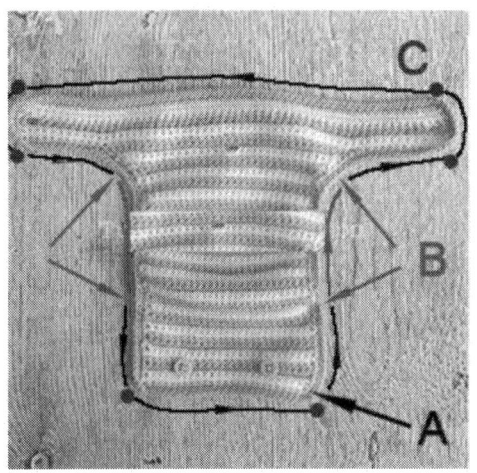

With Blue yarn:

Continue from where you end at diaper pants, a.k.a point A in the picture.

Round 1: ch, sc in next 12 sts (until you reach the red zone, point B). sc2 together in the next 30 sts (until you reach the end of the red zone). sc in next 17 sts (until you reach the bottom-right corner "blue dot" of the tab). 3sc in the corner st. sc in next st, 2sc in next hdc st, sc in next 2 sts (until you reach the top-right corner "blue dot" of the tab). 3sc in the corner st. sc in next 58 sts (until you reach the top-left corner "blue dot" of the tab). 3sc in the corner st. sc in next 2 sts, 2sc in next ch space, sc in next st (until you reach the bottom-left corner "blue dot" of the tab). 3sc in the corner st. sc in next 17 sts (until you reach the red zone on the left-hand side). sc2 together in the next 30 sts (until you reach the end of the red zone). sc in next 11 sts (until you reach the bottom-left corner "blue dot" of the diaper pants). 3sc in the corner st. sc in next 24 sts (until you reach the bottom-right corner of the diaper pants). 2 sc in the first st of the round. slst to the top loops of the first sc of the round.

Round 2: ch, sc in each st around, except the middle st of the corner stitches. sc in the middle st of the 3sc that you have done on the blue dots marking.

Fasten off. Hide yarn

Wear the diaper pants on the elephant and mark the positions for the buttons. Sew 2 small buttons as the fastener of the diaper pants.

Animals Amigurumi

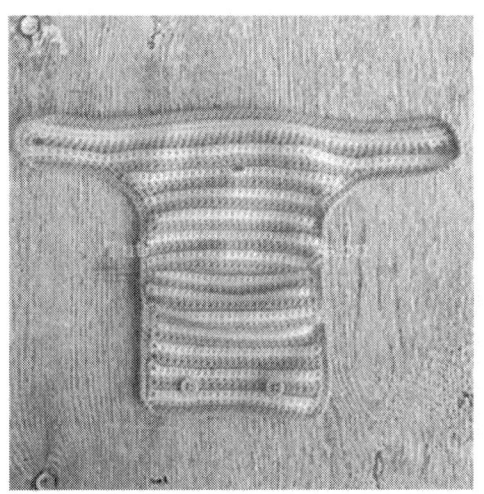

Complete with edging and buttons.

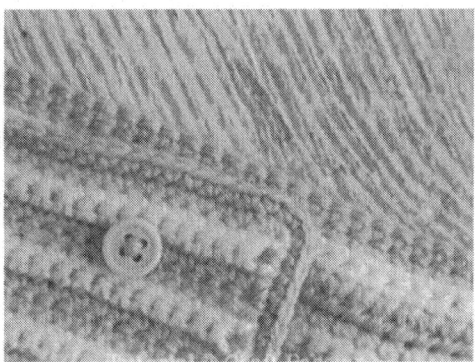

#

DRESS (WITH BODY)

Ruffles trim for the skirt of the dress

Round 1: ch 64 loosely or use 1 size bigger crochet hook. slst to the first ch to make a ring. {64}

Round 2: ch3 (as 1 dc), dc in the same st, 2dc in next 63 sts, slst to the first st of the round. {128}

Round 3: ch, sc around. {128}

Round 4: ch3 (as 1 dc), dc in the same st, 2dc in next 127 sts, slst to the first st of the round. {256}

Collar ruffles trim

Round 1: ch 36 loosely or use 1 size bigger crochet hook. slst to the first ch to make a ring. {36}

Round 2: ch, 2sc in next 36 sts, slst to the first st of the round. {72}

Round 3: {ch3, sc in next st} in next 72 sts. slst to the first st of the round.

Work body pattern until you completed round17. Change yarn to rainbow color.

Add bottom ruffles to the body at round18 by sc the base of the ruffle piece to the body.

Continue to crochet the body with rainbow yarn until round 36.

Change yarn to Cyan color.

Add collar ruffles trim to the body at round37 by crochet the base of the ruffle piece to the body by using cyan yarn.

Fasten off. Hide yarn

#

How to assembly the Elephant Amigurumi

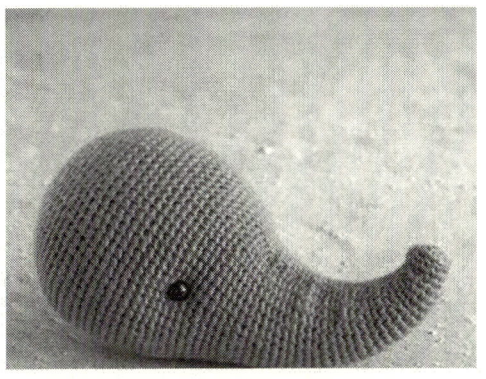

Sew 2 black buttons as eyes at round 38, at the center of each side of the head; roughly 27 stitches apart.

Do not cut the yarn after sewing the first eye, instead, insert it into the head and come out from the second eye to sew another eye.

Pull the yarn a little to sink the eyes into the head, knot securely. You can run the yarn through the head a few times to prevent the yarn from snapping in the long run.

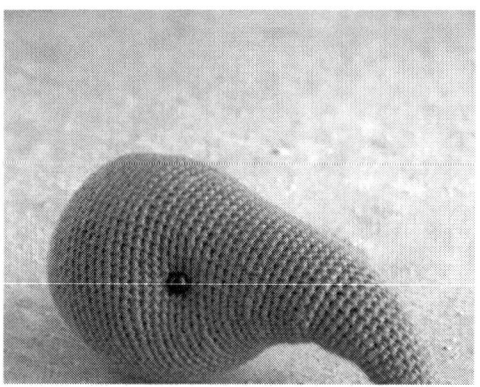

If you turn the head the other way round, it is the trunk down expression.

Elwis is with the trunk pointing upward, Elyra is with the trunk pointing downward.

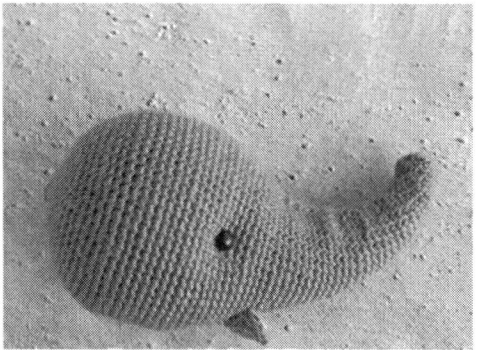

If you are making Elwis with the trunk-up position, sew the mouth between round 33 to 36.

Another view after the mouth is sewn.

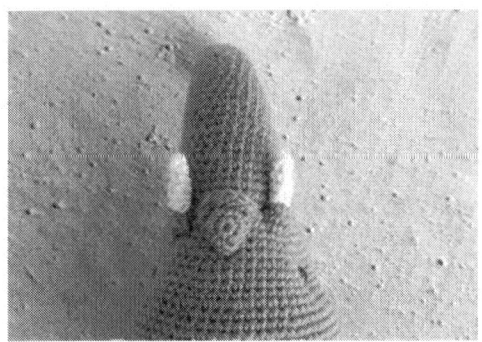

(bottom view)

Followed by sewing the tusks between round 32 to 34, 7 stitches apart at the sides of the mouth.

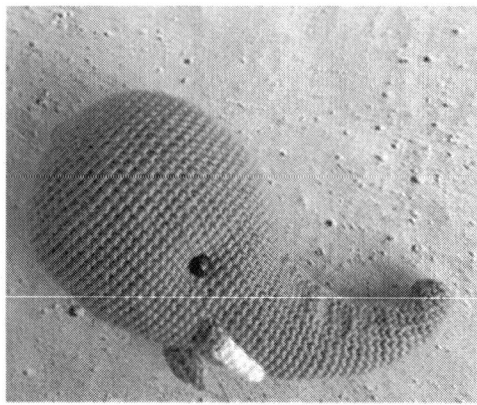

The side view after the eyes, mouth, and tusks are sewed to the head.

Sew the ears and body to the head followed by sewing arms (between head and body), feet (on round 14), and tail (on round 16) to the body to complete the elephant amigurumi.

Animals Amigurumi

Made in the USA
Las Vegas, NV
26 February 2021